WINE NOTES

WINE NOTES

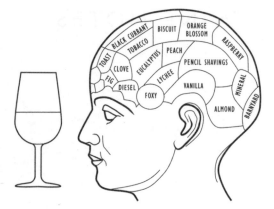

Wine is like music – it's nice in the background, but if you want to learn about it, a little focus is necessary.

WINE TASTING NOTEBOOK
By Steve De Long

ISBN 0-9723632-5-4
Printed in China
© 2008 De Long Company

TABLE OF CONTENTS

Introduction   4

How to Take a Wine Tasting Note   6

    Appearance   7

    Aroma   8

    Palate   9

    Wrapping it Up   11

Sample Tasting Notes   12

    Red - Côtes du Rhône   12

    White - Sauvignon Blanc   13

Vintage Chart   14

Varietally Correct?   16

Wine Tasting Note Forms   17

Wine Tasting Terms   endpaper
                                            pull-out

For more information on wine tasting,
please visit www.delongwine.com.

Special thanks to: Tyler Colman, Deborah
De Long, Michael Gitter, Richard Leahy, Eric
Lecours, Toby Riddel, Arthur Stein and Ben
Schmerler for their invaluable input

INTRODUCTION

If you're interested in getting better treatment in a restaurant or tasting room, I know of one sure way: take notes. Faster than you can say "expert in the house", the staff will be falling all over you, indulging your every whim. OK, I'm exaggerating. The real reason to take wine notes is that it's the fastest and most effective way to improve your knowledge of wine.

Much like music, we can conveniently relegate wine to the background without really thinking about it. This is perfectly fine. Wine and song make most things better, but you aren't going to learn about either without a little focus. Consider the brain activity of a sommelier vs. a casual wine drinker when imbibing a glass of wine. The sommelier's brain scan will show lots of activity in the frontal lobe—the region of the brain where perception, language, interpretation, etc., occur—while the casual wine drinker will have little brain activity measured at all. The sommelier is taking a note even if nothing is written down.

It's ironic how sommeliers and wine connoisseurs are leading the charge back to regaining our primitive sense of taste and smell (when we talk about *wine tasting* we're really talking about *wine tasting* and *smelling*). Both have been severely devalued over the centuries as we no longer rely on them for our survival. Modern people are actually embarrassed by their sense of smell—have you ever heard of anyone getting a nose enlargement? Viva les sommeliers! Let's use it before we lose it!

Smell is a powerful sense in the way it can trigger long-forgotten memories. You catch a whiff of something familiar but strange—"that's what Grandma's house smelled like"—and you're vividly transported back to Grandma's house for a few moments. In the same way, the smell memory you get from tasting and thinking about different wines can trigger memories like: "this Côtes du Rhône tastes something like the Minervois we had a few months ago". The mental catalogue you compile is the basis of any wine taster's expertise and when written down greatly accelerates your understanding of wine. It also takes very little writing time for each wine tasted—time well spent for a special bottle or one you would like to remember.

No matter what form wine tasting notes take—purely committed to memory, scrawled on the back of a napkin or business card, or written on a standardized note sheet—they all share the same basic format. All take into account what the wine looks, smells, and tastes like. You may find wine tasting notes—even the florid treatments of some experts—pretty boring. Let's face it: they're more like a cross between a diary entry and a shopping list—personal notes and reminders—than like great (or even good) prose. You shouldn't feel pressured to write anything more than a useful reminder of your tasting experience.

Personally, I like the standardized forms since they add a sense of discipline I don't usually have. Remember: you're drinking when you do this!

Cheers!

Steve De Long

WINE TASTING NOTE

This standardized tasting note form has been developed for beginners and professionals alike. For beginners, it provides a framework to record impressions in a meaningful way. For professionals, it puts the repetitive parts of a note in quick multiple-choice selections while still allowing some flexibility.

If this is your first tasting note or if you've never taken a standardized tasting note, the form may look a little daunting. Don't let it put you off – the fundamentals aren't difficult. Indeed, after a few notes, you can be tasting like a pro.

WHAT YOU'LL NEED:

+ Wine, of course! One of the best ways to accelerate your wine tasting ability is to compare two or more wines at one time.
+ A tulip-shaped wine glass. The tulip shape concentrates the aroma to make it more pronounced. Fill the glass(es) to the approximate level shown at right.
+ A relaxed and open mind. Relaxation is critical to concentration.

As we go through the tasting note, please refer to the example notes on pages 12 and 13.

BACKGROUND INFORMATION

Before we taste, let's take care of the information on the top of the tasting note form. Wine labels often require a bit of deciphering, so if you're stuck, please visit www.delongwine.com/labels for assistance.

tasting date, location and tasting partner(s): These can be helpful in triggering your smell memory.

wine name: Wines don't always have a proprietary name (e.g., *Insignia, Tignanello*) in addition to producer and region (e.g., *Guigal Côtes du Rhône, Anti-*

nori Chianti Classico, etc.), so sometimes this part of the form is simply left blank.

producer: Usually this is front and center on the label, but it can be surprisingly difficult to locate.

region/appellation: This part is sometimes confused with the grape variety (i.e., wines from the region *Chablis* are made from the grape variety *Chardonnay*).

grape varieties: Sometimes this requires a little research such as visiting the producer's website.

vintage, alcohol, price: All useful pieces of information.

◉ APPEARANCE

Let's take a look at the wine. Hold your glass against a white background such as a tablecloth or piece of paper.

COLOUR HUE: Wines have a wide range of hues from pale green to amber in whites to purple-red to brown in reds. The hue of a young wine can give some indication of the grape variety it came from (i.e., *Barbera* – ruby, *Riesling* – pale green, *Chenin Blanc* – yellow, etc.). With age these hues change due to gradual oxidation. Over time red wines become brick and then brown, while white wines become more amber and rosés become more copper coloured.

COLOUR DEPTH: The intensity of colour depth also varies widely. Red wines get lighter with age while white wines tend to get darker.

CLARITY: Clarity used to be of utmost importance since lack thereof indicated spoilage. Since many wines are now unfiltered and may have a slight haze of sediment, only marked cloudiness indicates spoilage.

Extra space is provided for additional notes on the wine's appearance, such as the mousse/bubbles in sparkling wine or the edge/rim in a still wine. In our example, a note about the rim has been added. This information is not absolutely necessary for beginners but can tell a little about the concentration of the solids in the wine. A narrow rim indicates a higher concentration.

꒕ AROMA

We're now going to smell the wine. Give the glass a big swirl to release the aromas above the surface of the wine and inhale as if you were smelling a flower.

If you sense something wrong, take a look at the FAULTS section on the opposite side of this sheet. If there's a fault in the wine, return the wine to where you purchased it and get a replacement bottle.

AROMA INTENSITY: Some wines are more aromatic than others, but serving temperature can also be a factor. When served too cool, they lack aroma intensity. As a general guideline, whites and rosés should be served at 47-50°F (8-10°C) while reds should be served at 58-65°F (14-18°C). If you want to maximize the aroma, serve any colour of wine at 65°F (18°C); but above this temperature, the aroma, or nose, may be dominated by the smell of evaporating alcohol.

DEVELOPMENT: The age of a wine can be detected in its colour, but also in its aroma. A young wine will usually have a fragrance that is associated with the grape variety it is made from. Tannic young red wines meant to age can seem CLOSED if consumed prematurely. With age, wines can take on more mature aromas such as TOBACCO and LEATHER while becoming softer and more complex. Most wines, however, aren't made to age and will simply become progressively less fruity and, at a certain point, un-drinkable.

AROMAS: The hard part. If you're just starting out, it may be difficult to describe the aroma. Take a look at the WINE TASTING TERMS on the other side of this page and remember, when in doubt go for the most general term (i.e., FLORAL instead of VIOLETS). For example, you don't need to describe *all* the in-gredients of a fruit salad. Just start with "fruit" and try to write down the more specific components in the order you perceive them. It takes practice and you'll get much better at describing what you smell the more you taste wines.

〰 PALATE

Time to taste: Take a good mouthful of wine and let it coat all parts of your tongue. Hold it in your mouth for 5-10 seconds. If you need to take another taste, remember to wait 30 seconds for your palate to clear.

DRY/SWEET: Fermentation converts grape sugars to alcohol; sweeter wines simply haven't been fully converted and have varying degrees of RESIDUAL SUG-AR. Many white wines and most red wines (that aren't fortified) are DRY but still have a tiny hint of sweet-ness due to the fruit and alcohol, without which they would be considered BONE DRY. Moving up the sweetness scale, many German *Rieslings* are OFF-DRY or slightly sweet (although they can be found in all sweetness levels), while dessert wines range from MEDIUM SWEET to VERY SWEET.

BODY: This is the weight of the wine on your pal-ate, due to the amount of alcohol, glycerol, residual sugar and extract (soluble solids). A common error for new wine tasters is to call all wines light-bodied – and relative to a milkshake, all wines *are* light-bodied. A very light-bodied wine will feel lighter than water in your mouth while a very full-bodied or heavy wine will feel more like *Port* (a rich fortified wine). A word of caution: Don't be fooled by TANNINS (see below).

ACIDITY: All wine is naturally acidic. Acidity can be sensed on the sides of the tongue with a slight tingling sensation. At higher levels, you will also start to salivate. The range goes from *tart* to *flabby*. *Flabby* gets its name from the "blah" sensation when there just isn't enough acid to stimulate the tongue. Red wines tend to be less acidic than white wines.

TANNINS: Red wines (and a few whites) get their colour and tannins from contact with grape skins during fermentation. Tannins can also come from oak barrels and are sensed on the top of the tongue. High, hard tannins will have a pronounced raspy drying effect which can confuse the sensation of weight – the drying on the tongue makes the wine seem lighter. Keep this in mind especially with young red wines. A high level of soft or round tannins will give an almost chewy texture to a wine.

FLAVOUR INTENSITY: The intensity on the palate is usually similar to the intensity on the nose. Some wines will disappoint with a lower level of palate intensity and a rare one will have a palate intensity that surpasses that of the nose.

FLAVOURS: The flavours sensed here will usually be similar to the aromas perceived on the nose. The difference here is that the flavours are now entering your nasal cavity from the back door via the rear of your mouth instead of directly through the nostrils. Again, concentrate on picking out a few of the major flavours. The initial flavours/sensations (or lack thereof) are called the ATTACK, followed by the MID PALATE, and then the FINISH after you spit or swallow.

FINISH: In addition to the FLAVOUR(S) on the FIN-

ISH, the length of a wine is often an indication of quality; the longer the better. This is fairly easy to determine with a little practise – it's just the amount of time it takes for the flavour intensity to drop off substantially after spitting or swallowing.

WRAPPING IT UP

CONCLUSION/BALANCE: CONCLUSIONS are your general assessments of the wine, of which BALANCE should play a part. Note here if any of the elements are out of balance, especially if in excess. Excess alcohol feels hot, excess acidity is sharply tart, excess tannins are very rough, and excess residual sugar is cloyingly sweet. Any other impressions – including the positive ones, of course! – should go here as well.

RATING: Ratings are a useful shorthand to determine how much a wine was enjoyed and if it should (or should not) be purchased

★ ☆ ☆ ☆ ☆ POOR
★ ★ ☆ ☆ ☆ FAIR
★ ★ ★ ☆ ☆ GOOD
★ ★ ★ ★ ☆ VERY GOOD
★ ★ ★ ★ ★ EXCELLENT

again. Use any scale you wish; however, the 5-star scale is recommended here for ease of use.

FOOD PAIRING: This is one of the most practical and useful parts of the note. To keep things simple, only the main dish is noted. Remember: If you consider wine a food, it makes pairing it less mysterious.

☺ That's it. If this was your first formal tasting note, congratulations! Don't be discouraged if you weren't able to sense even half of what was discussed. You'll get better each time you taste.

For more instruction and guided tasting notes, please visit www.delongwine.com/notes

tasting date: *Sept 30 '08*   location: *Home*

tasting partner(s): *Deborah*

wine name: *Belleruche*

producer: *M. Chapoutier*

region/appellation: *Côtes-du-Rhône Rouge*

grape varieties: *Grenache 80%, Syrah 20%*

vintage: *2006*   alcohol: *14%*   price: *$10.99*

COLOUR HUE:
WHITE: greenish | yellow | straw yellow | gold | amber
RED: purplish | (ruby) red | garnet | brick | brown
ROSÉ: pink | salmon | orange | copper

COLOUR DEPTH:
watery | pale | (medium) deep | dark

CLARITY:
(clear) slight haze | cloudy

w/ narrow magenta rim

AROMA INTENSITY:
low | (moderate) aromatic | powerful

DEVELOPMENT:
(youthful) some age | aged

AROMAS:
earthy, spicy, raspberry/blackberry w/light
floral-violets.
something meaty as well

DRY/SWEET:
bone dry | (dry) off dry | medium sweet | sweet | very sweet

BODY:
very light | light | medium | medium-full | (full-bodied) heavy

ACIDITY:
tart | crisp | (lively) smooth | flabby

TANNINS (IF PRESENT):
LEVEL: (low) medium | high   TYPE: soft | (round) dry | hard

FLAVOUR INTENSITY:
weak | (moderate) flavourful | powerful

FLAVOURS:
spicy meaty, soft, earthy, raspberry blackberry
violets again
peppery finish

FINISH:
short (< 3 sec) | (medium (4-5)) long (5-7) | v. long (>8 sec)

CONCLUSION / BALANCE
A little hot on the alcohol but otherwise well
balanced - an enjoyable classic Côtes-du-
Rhône

rating: ★ ★ ★ ☆ ☆

FOOD: *roast chicken*

FOOD PAIRING:
MATCH: perfect | good | (neutral) bad

tasting date: *Oct 2 '08* location: *Home*

tasting partner(s): *Deborah*

wine name: *Private Bin*

producer: *Villa Maria*

region/appellation: *Marlborough*

grape varieties: *Sauvignon Blanc*

vintage: *2008* alcohol: *13%* price: *$13.99*

COLOUR HUE:
WHITE: (greenish) yellow | straw yellow | gold | amber
RED: purplish | ruby | red | garnet | brick | brown
ROSÉ: pink | salmon | orange | copper

COLOUR DEPTH:
(watery) pale | medium | deep | dark

CLARITY:
(clear) slight haze | cloudy

AROMA INTENSITY:
low | moderate | (aromatic) powerful

DEVELOPMENT:
(youthful) some age | aged

AROMAS:

gooseberry, mown-grass and citrus

DRY/SWEET:
bone dry | (dry) off dry | medium sweet | sweet | very sweet

BODY:
very light | light | (medium) medium-full | full-bodied | heavy

ACIDITY:
tart | (crisp) lively | smooth | flabby

TANNINS (IF PRESENT):
LEVEL: low | medium | high TYPE: soft | round | dry | hard

FLAVOUR INTENSITY:
weak | moderate | (flavourful) powerful

FLAVOURS:

very, very fruity gooseberries with fresh-mown grass and a spritz of lemon zest

---

FINISH:
short (< 3 sec) | (medium (4-5)) long (5-7) | v. long (>8 sec)

CONCLUSION / BALANCE

Very well balanced and flavorful - textbook clean and fruity New Zealand Sauv. Blanc

rating: ★ ★ ★ ☆ ☆

FOOD: *trout* **FOOD PAIRING:**
MATCH: (perfect) good | neutral | bad

VINTAGE

		2006	2005	2004	2003	2002	2001	2000	1999	1998
F R A N C E	Alsace	2	4	4	3	4	4	4	3	4
	Beaujolais	3	5	3	4	2	2	4	4	3
	Bordeaux - Red	4	5	4	4	4	4	5	4	4
	Bordeaux - Sauternes	4	5	3	5	4	5	4	4	4
	Burgundy - Red	4	5	3	4	5	3	3	5	3
	Burgundy - White	4	5	4	3	5	3	4	4	3
	Champagne	3	3	4	3	4	1	3	3	4
	Loire Valley	3	5	4	4	5	3	3	3	3
	Rhône - North	4	5	3	5	2	4	4	5	4
	Rhône - South	4	5	4	4	1	4	5	4	5
S P A I N	Priorat	4	5	5	4	3	5	5	4	5
	Rioja	4	5	5	3	3	5	3	3	3
	Ribera del Duero	3	4	5	4	3	5	4	5	4
ITALY	Piedmont	4	4	5	3	1	5	5	5	4
	Tuscany	5	4	5	4	1	5	4	5	4
	Vintage Port	2	5	4	4	2	3	5		3
	Germany - Riesling	4	5	4	4	4	5	3	4	4
	Austria	4	3	3	4	3	4	4	5	3
	Australia - Barrossa	4	5	4	4	5	4	3	3	5
	New Zealand	4	3	3	2	5	4	4	4	5
	Argentina	4	4	4	4	4	4	4	4	2
	Chile	4	5	4	4	3	5	4	2	4
	South Africa	5	3	4	5	4	5	3	3	4
U S A	California - Northern	4	4	4	4	4	4	3	4	3
	California - Central Coast	3	4	5	4	5	4	4	4	4
	Oregon	4	4	4	4	5	4	4	5	4
	Washington	5	5	4	4	4	4	4	4	4

KEY 5 Excellent
4 Very Good
3 Good
2 Fair
1 Poor

CHART

1997	1996	1995	1994	1993	1992	1991	1990	1989	1988	1987	Older exceptional vintages
5	4	3	3	3	3	2	5	5	5	3	'83,'76,'71,'61,'59
4	3	4	4	3	2	3	3	4	3	3	'82,'75,'61
3	4	4	4	3	1	1	5	5	4	2	'85,'82,'75,'61,'59,'53
4	4	4	2	1	1	1	5	5	4	1	'83,'75,'67,'59,'55,'49,'47
3	4	4	2	4	2	3	5	4	4	3	'78,'69,'59,'49,'45
4	5	5	3	3	4	2	4	4	3	2	'86,'66,'62,'47
3	4	5	2	3	3	2	5	4	5	1	'85,'82,'71,'64,'59,'52
4	4	4	3	3	2	2	5	5	4	2	'76,'71,'64,'59,'49,'47
4	4	4	3	1	2	4	5	5	4	3	'85,'83,'78,'71,'69,'61
3	3	4	3	3	2	2	5	5	4	2	'85,'83,'78,'70,'61
3	5	5	4	5	4	3	3	3	3	3	'80,'82,'85
3	4	5	5	3	3	4	3	3	3	4	'87,'85,'82,'78,'75,'70,'68
3	5	5	4	2	3	4	3	5	3	3	'86,'81
5	5	4	2	3	1	2	5	5	4	3	'85,'82,'78,'75,'68,'65,'62
5	2	4	3	4	1	3	5	1	5	2	'85,'82,'75,'71,'70, '67,'64
4	2	2	5		4	4				3	'76,'70,'66,'63,'55,'45
4	3	4	4	4	4	3	5	4	4	2	'76,'75,'71,'64,'59,'53
5	2	4	4	3	3	1	5	3	4	3	'86,'85,'69,'47
3	5	4	4	2	3	4	4	2	3	2	'86,'82,'76,'71,'63,'59
4	4	3	4	2	3	4	3	4	2	1	
4	4	5	3	4	3	3	4	4	3	3	
5	4	4	2	3	3	3	4	3	3	3	
3	2	4	3	3	4	3	2	2	4	5	
5	4	4	5	4	4	4	4	3	3	4	'85,'74,'69,'68,'65,'58,'51
4	4	4	4	3	4	4	4	4	4	4	
3	3	2	5	4	4	4	4	4	4	2	'83,'75
3	3	3	4	4	4	3	4	4	4	4	'83

Vintage charts are helpful to jog your memory or satisfy your curiosity about what years were *generally* best in a particular region. They're less useful in helping select a specific wine as good producers can make decent wines even in in poor years.

VARIETALLY CORRECT?

Grape varieties can be identified by certain characteristics. The following is a useful shorthand for the most common descriptors of popular grape varieties.

WHITE GRAPE VARIETIES

ALBARIÑO: lemons, tropical fruits

CHENIN BLANC: honey, lemon, wax, wet wool, quince

CHARDONNAY: white fruits (cool climates), tropical fruits (warm climates), vanilla (oaked)

GARGANEGA (THE SOAVE GRAPE): lemons, almonds, white fruits

GEWÜRZTRAMINER: lychees, spice

GRÜNER VELTLINER: white pepper, lentil, grapefruit

PINOT GRIS: white fruits, spice

PINOT BLANC: green apples

RIESLING: apple, honey, petrol

SAUVIGNON BLANC: grass, gooseberries, aromatic

VIOGNIER: apricots, exotic perfume, spice

RED GRAPE VARIETIES

CABERNET FRANC: blackcurrant, green pepper, pencil shavings

CABERNET SAUVIGNON: blackcurrant, anise, cedar

GAMAY: strawberry, banana

GRENACHE: berries, anise, white pepper

MERLOT: plums, chocolate, soft tannins

NEBBIOLO: rose, tar, truffles

PINOT NOIR: red fruits, fall leaves, horseradish

SANGIOVESE: sour cherries, tomatoes, clove

SYRAH/SHIRAZ: black pepper, black fruits

TEMPRANILLO: strawberry, oak, coconut, spice

ZINFANDEL: black cherry, blackberry

tasting date: location:

tasting partner(s):

wine name:

producer:

region/appellation:

grape varieties:

vintage: alcohol: price:

COLOUR HUE:
WHITE: greenish | yellow | straw yellow | gold | amber
RED: purple | ruby | red | garnet | brick | brown
ROSÉ: pink | salmon | orange | copper

COLOUR DEPTH:
watery | pale | medium | deep | dark

CLARITY:
clear | slight haze | cloudy

AROMA INTENSITY:
low | moderate | aromatic | powerful

DEVELOPMENT:
youthful | some age | aged

AROMAS:

DRY/SWEET:
bone dry | dry | off dry | medium sweet | sweet | very sweet

BODY:
very light | light | medium | medium-full | full-bodied | heavy

ACIDITY:
tart | crisp | lively | smooth | flabby

TANNINS (IF PRESENT):
LEVEL: low | medium | high   TYPE: soft | round | dry | hard

FLAVOUR INTENSITY:
low | moderate | flavourful | powerful

FLAVOURS:

FINISH:
short (< 3 sec) | medium (4-5) | long (5-7) | v. long (>8 sec)

CONCLUSION/BALANCE:

rating:

FOOD: **FOOD PAIRING:**

MATCH: perfect | good | neutral | bad

tasting date: location:

tasting partner(s):

wine name:

producer:

region/appellation:

grape varieties:

vintage: alcohol: price:

COLOUR HUE:
WHITE: greenish | yellow | straw yellow | gold | amber
RED: purple | ruby | red | garnet | brick | brown
ROSÉ: pink | salmon | orange | copper

COLOUR DEPTH:
watery | pale | medium | deep | dark

CLARITY:
clear | slight haze | cloudy

AROMA INTENSITY:
low | moderate | aromatic | powerful

DEVELOPMENT:
youthful | some age | aged

AROMAS:

DRY/SWEET:
bone dry | dry | off dry | medium sweet | sweet | very sweet

BODY:
very light | light | medium | medium-full | full-bodied | heavy

ACIDITY:
tart | crisp | lively | smooth | flabby

TANNINS (IF PRESENT):
LEVEL: low | medium | high   TYPE: soft | round | dry | hard

FLAVOUR INTENSITY:
low | moderate | flavourful | powerful

FLAVOURS:

FINISH:
short (< 3 sec) | medium (4-5) | long (5-7) | v. long (>8 sec)

CONCLUSION/BALANCE:

rating:

FOOD: **FOOD PAIRING:**
                    MATCH: perfect | good | neutral | bad

tasting date: location:

tasting partner(s):

wine name:

producer:

region/appellation:

grape varieties:

vintage: alcohol: price:

COLOUR HUE:

WHITE: greenish | yellow | straw yellow | gold | amber
RED: purple | ruby | red | garnet | brick | brown
ROSÉ: pink | salmon | orange | copper

COLOUR DEPTH:
watery | pale | medium | deep | dark

CLARITY:
clear | slight haze | cloudy

AROMA INTENSITY:
low | moderate | aromatic | powerful

DEVELOPMENT:
youthful | some age | aged

AROMAS:

DRY/SWEET:
bone dry | dry | off dry | medium sweet | sweet | very sweet

BODY:
very light | light | medium | medium-full | full-bodied | heavy

ACIDITY:
tart | crisp | lively | smooth | flabby

TANNINS (IF PRESENT):
LEVEL: low | medium | high   TYPE: soft | round | dry | hard

FLAVOUR INTENSITY:
low | moderate | flavourful | powerful

FLAVOURS:

FINISH:
short (< 3 sec) | medium (4-5) | long (5-7) | v. long (>8 sec)

CONCLUSION/BALANCE:

rating:

FOOD: **FOOD PAIRING:**
               MATCH: perfect | good | neutral | bad

tasting date: location:

tasting partner(s):

wine name:

producer:

region/appellation:

grape varieties:

vintage: alcohol: price:

COLOUR HUE:

WHITE: greenish | yellow | straw yellow | gold | amber
RED: purple | ruby | red | garnet | brick | brown
ROSÉ: pink | salmon | orange | copper

COLOUR DEPTH:
watery | pale | medium | deep | dark

CLARITY:
clear | slight haze | cloudy

AROMA INTENSITY:
low | moderate | aromatic | powerful

DEVELOPMENT:
youthful | some age | aged

AROMAS:

DRY/SWEET:
bone dry | dry | off dry | medium sweet | sweet | very sweet

BODY:
very light | light | medium | medium-full | full-bodied | heavy

ACIDITY:
tart | crisp | lively | smooth | flabby

TANNINS (IF PRESENT):
LEVEL: low | medium | high   TYPE: soft | round | dry | hard

FLAVOUR INTENSITY:
low | moderate | flavourful | powerful

FLAVOURS:

FINISH:
short (< 3 sec) | medium (4-5) | long (5-7) | v. long (>8 sec)

CONCLUSION/BALANCE:

rating:

FOOD: **FOOD PAIRING:**
                        MATCH: perfect | good | neutral | bad

tasting date: location:

tasting partner(s):

wine name:

producer:

region/appellation:

grape varieties:

vintage: alcohol: price:

COLOUR HUE:
WHITE: greenish | yellow | straw yellow | gold | amber
RED: purple | ruby | red | garnet | brick | brown
ROSÉ: pink | salmon | orange | copper

COLOUR DEPTH:
watery | pale | medium | deep | dark

CLARITY:
clear | slight haze | cloudy

AROMA INTENSITY:
low | moderate | aromatic | powerful

DEVELOPMENT:
youthful | some age | aged

AROMAS:

DRY/SWEET:
bone dry | dry | off dry | medium sweet | sweet | very sweet

BODY:
very light | light | medium | medium-full | full-bodied | heavy

ACIDITY:
tart | crisp | lively | smooth | flabby

TANNINS (IF PRESENT):
LEVEL: low | medium | high TYPE: soft | round | dry | hard

FLAVOUR INTENSITY:
low | moderate | flavourful | powerful

FLAVOURS:

FINISH:
short (< 3 sec) | medium (4-5) | long (5-7) | v. long (>8 sec)

CONCLUSION/BALANCE:

rating:

FOOD: **FOOD PAIRING:**
MATCH: perfect | good | neutral | bad

tasting date: location:

tasting partner(s):

wine name:

producer:

region/appellation:

grape varieties:

vintage: alcohol: price:

COLOUR HUE:
WHITE: greenish | yellow | straw yellow | gold | amber
RED: purple | ruby | red | garnet | brick | brown
ROSÉ: pink | salmon | orange | copper

COLOUR DEPTH:
watery | pale | medium | deep | dark

CLARITY:
clear | slight haze | cloudy

AROMA INTENSITY:
low | moderate | aromatic | powerful

DEVELOPMENT:
youthful | some age | aged

AROMAS:

DRY/SWEET:
bone dry | dry | off dry | medium sweet | sweet | very sweet

BODY:
very light | light | medium | medium-full | full-bodied | heavy

ACIDITY:
tart | crisp | lively | smooth | flabby

TANNINS (IF PRESENT):
LEVEL: low | medium | high   TYPE: soft | round | dry | hard

FLAVOUR INTENSITY:
low | moderate | flavourful | powerful

FLAVOURS:

FINISH:
short (< 3 sec) | medium (4-5) | long (5-7) | v. long (>8 sec)

CONCLUSION/BALANCE:

rating:

FOOD: **FOOD PAIRING:**
                  MATCH: perfect | good | neutral | bad

tasting date: location:

tasting partner(s):

wine name:

producer:

region/appellation:

grape varieties:

vintage: alcohol: price:

COLOUR HUE:
WHITE: greenish | yellow | straw yellow | gold | amber
RED: purple | ruby | red | garnet | brick | brown
ROSÉ: pink | salmon | orange | copper

COLOUR DEPTH:
watery | pale | medium | deep | dark

CLARITY:
clear | slight haze | cloudy

AROMA INTENSITY:
low | moderate | aromatic | powerful

DEVELOPMENT:
youthful | some age | aged

AROMAS:

DRY/SWEET:
bone dry | dry | off dry | medium sweet | sweet | very sweet

BODY:
very light | light | medium | medium-full | full-bodied | heavy

ACIDITY:
tart | crisp | lively | smooth | flabby

TANNINS (IF PRESENT):
LEVEL: low | medium | high   TYPE: soft | round | dry | hard

FLAVOUR INTENSITY:
low | moderate | flavourful | powerful

FLAVOURS:

FINISH:
short (< 3 sec) | medium (4-5) | long (5-7) | v. long (>8 sec)

CONCLUSION/BALANCE:

rating:

FOOD: **FOOD PAIRING:**

MATCH: perfect | good | neutral | bad

tasting date: location:

tasting partner(s):

wine name:

producer:

region/appellation:

grape varieties:

vintage: alcohol: price:

COLOUR HUE:
WHITE: greenish | yellow | straw yellow | gold | amber
RED: purple | ruby | red | garnet | brick | brown
ROSÉ: pink | salmon | orange | copper

COLOUR DEPTH:
watery | pale | medium | deep | dark

CLARITY:
clear | slight haze | cloudy

AROMA INTENSITY:
low | moderate | aromatic | powerful

DEVELOPMENT:
youthful | some age | aged

AROMAS:

DRY/SWEET:
bone dry | dry | off dry | medium sweet | sweet | very sweet

BODY:
very light | light | medium | medium-full | full-bodied | heavy

ACIDITY:
tart | crisp | lively | smooth | flabby

TANNINS (IF PRESENT):
LEVEL: low | medium | high   TYPE: soft | round | dry | hard

FLAVOUR INTENSITY:
low | moderate | flavourful | powerful

FLAVOURS:

FINISH:
short (< 3 sec) | medium (4-5) | long (5-7) | v. long (>8 sec)

CONCLUSION/BALANCE:

rating:

FOOD: **FOOD PAIRING:**
                     MATCH: perfect | good | neutral | bad

tasting date: location:

tasting partner(s):

wine name:

producer:

region/appellation:

grape varieties:

vintage: alcohol: price:

COLOUR HUE:

WHITE: greenish | yellow | straw yellow | gold | amber
RED: purple | ruby | red | garnet | brick | brown
ROSÉ: pink | salmon | orange | copper

COLOUR DEPTH:
watery | pale | medium | deep | dark

CLARITY:
clear | slight haze | cloudy

AROMA INTENSITY:
low | moderate | aromatic | powerful

DEVELOPMENT:
youthful | some age | aged

AROMAS:

DRY/SWEET:
bone dry | dry | off dry | medium sweet | sweet | very sweet

BODY:
very light | light | medium | medium-full | full-bodied | heavy

ACIDITY:
tart | crisp | lively | smooth | flabby

TANNINS (IF PRESENT):
LEVEL: low | medium | high   TYPE: soft | round | dry | hard

FLAVOUR INTENSITY:
low | moderate | flavourful | powerful

FLAVOURS:

FINISH:
short (< 3 sec) | medium (4-5) | long (5-7) | v. long (>8 sec)

CONCLUSION/BALANCE:

rating:

FOOD: ## FOOD PAIRING:
MATCH: perfect | good | neutral | bad

tasting date: location:

tasting partner(s):

wine name:

producer:

region/appellation:

grape varieties:

vintage: alcohol: price:

COLOUR HUE:
WHITE: greenish | yellow | straw yellow | gold | amber
RED: purple | ruby | red | garnet | brick | brown
ROSÉ: pink | salmon | orange | copper

COLOUR DEPTH:
watery | pale | medium | deep | dark

CLARITY:
clear | slight haze | cloudy

AROMA INTENSITY:
low | moderate | aromatic | powerful

DEVELOPMENT:
youthful | some age | aged

AROMAS:

DRY/SWEET:
bone dry | dry | off dry | medium sweet | sweet | very sweet

BODY:
very light | light | medium | medium-full | full-bodied | heavy

ACIDITY:
tart | crisp | lively | smooth | flabby

TANNINS (IF PRESENT):
LEVEL: low | medium | high   TYPE: soft | round | dry | hard

FLAVOUR INTENSITY:
low | moderate | flavourful | powerful

FLAVOURS:

FINISH:
short (< 3 sec) | medium (4-5) | long (5-7) | v. long (>8 sec)

CONCLUSION/BALANCE:

rating:

FOOD: **FOOD PAIRING:**
                 MATCH: perfect | good | neutral | bad

tasting date: location:

tasting partner(s):

wine name:

producer:

region/appellation:

grape varieties:

vintage: alcohol: price:

COLOUR HUE:

WHITE: greenish | yellow | straw yellow | gold | amber
RED: purple | ruby | red | garnet | brick | brown
ROSÉ: pink | salmon | orange | copper

COLOUR DEPTH:
watery | pale | medium | deep | dark

CLARITY:
clear | slight haze | cloudy

AROMA INTENSITY:
low | moderate | aromatic | powerful

DEVELOPMENT:
youthful | some age | aged

AROMAS:

DRY/SWEET:
bone dry | dry | off dry | medium sweet | sweet | very sweet

BODY:
very light | light | medium | medium-full | full-bodied | heavy

ACIDITY:
tart | crisp | lively | smooth | flabby

TANNINS (IF PRESENT):
LEVEL: low | medium | high   TYPE: soft | round | dry | hard

FLAVOUR INTENSITY:
low | moderate | flavourful | powerful

FLAVOURS:

FINISH:
short (< 3 sec) | medium (4-5) | long (5-7) | v. long (>8 sec)

CONCLUSION/BALANCE:

rating:

FOOD: **FOOD PAIRING:**
                  MATCH: perfect | good | neutral | bad

tasting date: location:

tasting partner(s):

wine name:

producer:

region/appellation:

grape varieties:

vintage: alcohol: price:

COLOUR HUE:
WHITE: greenish | yellow | straw yellow | gold | amber
RED: purple | ruby | red | garnet | brick | brown
ROSÉ: pink | salmon | orange | copper

COLOUR DEPTH:
watery | pale | medium | deep | dark

CLARITY:
clear | slight haze | cloudy

AROMA INTENSITY:
low | moderate | aromatic | powerful

DEVELOPMENT:
youthful | some age | aged

AROMAS:

DRY/SWEET:
bone dry | dry | off dry | medium sweet | sweet | very sweet

BODY:
very light | light | medium | medium-full | full-bodied | heavy

ACIDITY:
tart | crisp | lively | smooth | flabby

TANNINS (IF PRESENT):
LEVEL: low | medium | high   TYPE: soft | round | dry | hard

FLAVOUR INTENSITY:
low | moderate | flavourful | powerful

FLAVOURS:

FINISH:
short (< 3 sec) | medium (4-5) | long (5-7) | v. long (>8 sec)

CONCLUSION/BALANCE:

rating:

FOOD: **FOOD PAIRING:**
                MATCH: perfect | good | neutral | bad

tasting date: location:

tasting partner(s):

wine name:

producer:

region/appellation:

grape varieties:

vintage: alcohol: price:

COLOUR HUE:

WHITE: greenish | yellow | straw yellow | gold | amber
RED: purple | ruby | red | garnet | brick | brown
ROSÉ: pink | salmon | orange | copper

COLOUR DEPTH:
watery | pale | medium | deep | dark

CLARITY:
clear | slight haze | cloudy

AROMA INTENSITY:
low | moderate | aromatic | powerful

DEVELOPMENT:
youthful | some age | aged

AROMAS:

DRY/SWEET:
bone dry | dry | off dry | medium sweet | sweet | very sweet

BODY:
very light | light | medium | medium-full | full-bodied | heavy

ACIDITY:
tart | crisp | lively | smooth | flabby

TANNINS (IF PRESENT):
LEVEL: low | medium | high   TYPE: soft | round | dry | hard

FLAVOUR INTENSITY:
low | moderate | flavourful | powerful

FLAVOURS:

FINISH:
short (< 3 sec) | medium (4-5) | long (5-7) | v. long (>8 sec)

CONCLUSION/BALANCE:

rating:

FOOD: **FOOD PAIRING:**

MATCH: perfect | good | neutral | bad

tasting date: location:

tasting partner(s):

wine name:

producer:

region/appellation:

grape varieties:

vintage: alcohol: price:

COLOUR HUE:
WHITE: greenish | yellow | straw yellow | gold | amber
RED: purple | ruby | red | garnet | brick | brown
ROSÉ: pink | salmon | orange | copper

COLOUR DEPTH:
watery | pale | medium | deep | dark

CLARITY:
clear | slight haze | cloudy

AROMA INTENSITY:
low | moderate | aromatic | powerful

DEVELOPMENT:
youthful | some age | aged

AROMAS:

DRY/SWEET:
bone dry | dry | off dry | medium sweet | sweet | very sweet

BODY:
very light | light | medium | medium-full | full-bodied | heavy

ACIDITY:
tart | crisp | lively | smooth | flabby

TANNINS (IF PRESENT):
LEVEL: low | medium | high   TYPE: soft | round | dry | hard

FLAVOUR INTENSITY:
low | moderate | flavourful | powerful

FLAVOURS:

FINISH:
short (< 3 sec) | medium (4-5) | long (5-7) | v. long (>8 sec)

CONCLUSION/BALANCE:

rating:

FOOD: **FOOD PAIRING:**

MATCH: perfect | good | neutral | bad

tasting date: location:

tasting partner(s):

wine name:

producer:

region/appellation:

grape varieties:

vintage: alcohol: price:

COLOUR HUE:
WHITE: greenish | yellow | straw yellow | gold | amber
RED: purple | ruby | red | garnet | brick | brown
ROSÉ: pink | salmon | orange | copper

COLOUR DEPTH:
watery | pale | medium | deep | dark

CLARITY:
clear | slight haze | cloudy

AROMA INTENSITY:
low | moderate | aromatic | powerful

DEVELOPMENT:
youthful | some age | aged

AROMAS:

DRY/SWEET:
bone dry | dry | off dry | medium sweet | sweet | very sweet

BODY:
very light | light | medium | medium-full | full-bodied | heavy

ACIDITY:
tart | crisp | lively | smooth | flabby

TANNINS (IF PRESENT):
LEVEL: low | medium | high   TYPE: soft | round | dry | hard

FLAVOUR INTENSITY:
low | moderate | flavourful | powerful

FLAVOURS:

FINISH:
short (< 3 sec) | medium (4-5) | long (5-7) | v. long (>8 sec)

CONCLUSION/BALANCE:

rating:

FOOD: **FOOD PAIRING:**
                MATCH: perfect | good | neutral | bad

tasting date: location:

tasting partner(s):

wine name:

producer:

region/appellation:

grape varieties:

vintage: alcohol: price:

COLOUR HUE:

WHITE: greenish | yellow | straw yellow | gold | amber
RED: purple | ruby | red | garnet | brick | brown
ROSÉ: pink | salmon | orange | copper

COLOUR DEPTH:
watery | pale | medium | deep | dark

CLARITY:
clear | slight haze | cloudy

AROMA INTENSITY:
low | moderate | aromatic | powerful

DEVELOPMENT:
youthful | some age | aged

AROMAS:

DRY/SWEET:
bone dry | dry | off dry | medium sweet | sweet | very sweet

BODY:
very light | light | medium | medium-full | full-bodied | heavy

ACIDITY:
tart | crisp | lively | smooth | flabby

TANNINS (IF PRESENT):
LEVEL: low | medium | high   TYPE: soft | round | dry | hard

FLAVOUR INTENSITY:
low | moderate | flavourful | powerful

FLAVOURS:

FINISH:
short (< 3 sec) | medium (4-5) | long (5-7) | v. long (>8 sec)

CONCLUSION/BALANCE:

rating:

FOOD: **FOOD PAIRING:**

MATCH: perfect | good | neutral | bad

tasting date: location:

tasting partner(s):

wine name:

producer:

region/appellation:

grape varieties:

vintage: alcohol: price:

COLOUR HUE:

WHITE: greenish | yellow | straw yellow | gold | amber
RED: purple | ruby | red | garnet | brick | brown
ROSÉ: pink | salmon | orange | copper

COLOUR DEPTH:
watery | pale | medium | deep | dark

CLARITY:
clear | slight haze | cloudy

AROMA INTENSITY:
low | moderate | aromatic | powerful

DEVELOPMENT:
youthful | some age | aged

AROMAS:

DRY/SWEET:
bone dry | dry | off dry | medium sweet | sweet | very sweet

BODY:
very light | light | medium | medium-full | full-bodied | heavy

ACIDITY:
tart | crisp | lively | smooth | flabby

TANNINS (IF PRESENT):
LEVEL: low | medium | high   TYPE: soft | round | dry | hard

FLAVOUR INTENSITY:
low | moderate | flavourful | powerful

FLAVOURS:

FINISH:
short (< 3 sec) | medium (4-5) | long (5-7) | v. long (>8 sec)

CONCLUSION/BALANCE:

rating:

FOOD: **FOOD PAIRING:**
                   MATCH: perfect | good | neutral | bad

tasting date: location:

tasting partner(s):

wine name:

producer:

region/appellation:

grape varieties:

vintage: alcohol: price:

COLOUR HUE:
WHITE: greenish | yellow | straw yellow | gold | amber
RED: purple | ruby | red | garnet | brick | brown
ROSÉ: pink | salmon | orange | copper

COLOUR DEPTH:
watery | pale | medium | deep | dark

CLARITY:
clear | slight haze | cloudy

AROMA INTENSITY:
low | moderate | aromatic | powerful

DEVELOPMENT:
youthful | some age | aged

AROMAS:

DRY/SWEET:
bone dry | dry | off dry | medium sweet | sweet | very sweet

BODY:
very light | light | medium | medium-full | full-bodied | heavy

ACIDITY:
tart | crisp | lively | smooth | flabby

TANNINS (IF PRESENT):
LEVEL: low | medium | high   TYPE: soft | round | dry | hard

FLAVOUR INTENSITY:
low | moderate | flavourful | powerful

FLAVOURS:

FINISH:
short (< 3 sec) | medium (4-5) | long (5-7) | v. long (>8 sec)

CONCLUSION/BALANCE:

rating:

FOOD: **FOOD PAIRING:**
                 MATCH: perfect | good | neutral | bad

tasting date: location:

tasting partner(s):

wine name:

producer:

region/appellation:

grape varieties:

vintage: alcohol: price:

COLOUR HUE:
WHITE: greenish | yellow | straw yellow | gold | amber
RED: purple | ruby | red | garnet | brick | brown
ROSÉ: pink | salmon | orange | copper

COLOUR DEPTH:
watery | pale | medium | deep | dark

CLARITY:
clear | slight haze | cloudy

AROMA INTENSITY:
low | moderate | aromatic | powerful

DEVELOPMENT:
youthful | some age | aged

AROMAS:

DRY/SWEET:
bone dry | dry | off dry | medium sweet | sweet | very sweet

BODY:
very light | light | medium | medium-full | full-bodied | heavy

ACIDITY:
tart | crisp | lively | smooth | flabby

TANNINS (IF PRESENT):
LEVEL: low | medium | high   TYPE: soft | round | dry | hard

FLAVOUR INTENSITY:
low | moderate | flavourful | powerful

FLAVOURS:

FINISH:
short (< 3 sec) | medium (4-5) | long (5-7) | v. long (>8 sec)

CONCLUSION/BALANCE:

rating:

FOOD: **FOOD PAIRING:**
                       MATCH: perfect | good | neutral | bad

tasting date: location:

tasting partner(s):

wine name:

producer:

region/appellation:

grape varieties:

vintage: alcohol: price:

COLOUR HUE:

WHITE: greenish | yellow | straw yellow | gold | amber
RED: purple | ruby | red | garnet | brick | brown
ROSÉ: pink | salmon | orange | copper

COLOUR DEPTH:
watery | pale | medium | deep | dark

CLARITY:
clear | slight haze | cloudy

AROMA INTENSITY:
low | moderate | aromatic | powerful

DEVELOPMENT:
youthful | some age | aged

AROMAS:

DRY/SWEET:
bone dry | dry | off dry | medium sweet | sweet | very sweet

BODY:
very light | light | medium | medium-full | full-bodied | heavy

ACIDITY:
tart | crisp | lively | smooth | flabby

TANNINS (IF PRESENT):
LEVEL: low | medium | high   TYPE: soft | round | dry | hard

FLAVOUR INTENSITY:
low | moderate | flavourful | powerful

FLAVOURS:

FINISH:
short (< 3 sec) | medium (4-5) | long (5-7) | v. long (>8 sec)

CONCLUSION/BALANCE:

rating:

FOOD: **FOOD PAIRING:**

MATCH: perfect | good | neutral | bad

tasting date: location:

tasting partner(s):

wine name:

producer:

region/appellation:

grape varieties:

vintage: alcohol: price:

COLOUR HUE:

WHITE: greenish | yellow | straw yellow | gold | amber
RED: purple | ruby | red | garnet | brick | brown
ROSÉ: pink | salmon | orange | copper

COLOUR DEPTH:
watery | pale | medium | deep | dark

CLARITY:
clear | slight haze | cloudy

AROMA INTENSITY:
low | moderate | aromatic | powerful

DEVELOPMENT:
youthful | some age | aged

AROMAS:

DRY/SWEET:
bone dry | dry | off dry | medium sweet | sweet | very sweet

BODY:
very light | light | medium | medium-full | full-bodied | heavy

ACIDITY:
tart | crisp | lively | smooth | flabby

TANNINS (IF PRESENT):
LEVEL: low | medium | high   TYPE: soft | round | dry | hard

FLAVOUR INTENSITY:
low | moderate | flavourful | powerful

FLAVOURS:

FINISH:
short (< 3 sec) | medium (4-5) | long (5-7) | v. long (>8 sec)

CONCLUSION/BALANCE:

rating:

FOOD: **FOOD PAIRING:**

MATCH: perfect | good | neutral | bad

tasting date: location:

tasting partner(s):

wine name:

producer:

region/appellation:

grape varieties:

vintage: alcohol: price:

COLOUR HUE:
WHITE: greenish | yellow | straw yellow | gold | amber
RED: purple | ruby | red | garnet | brick | brown
ROSÉ: pink | salmon | orange | copper

COLOUR DEPTH:
watery | pale | medium | deep | dark

CLARITY:
clear | slight haze | cloudy

AROMA INTENSITY:
low | moderate | aromatic | powerful

DEVELOPMENT:
youthful | some age | aged

AROMAS:

DRY/SWEET:
bone dry | dry | off dry | medium sweet | sweet | very sweet

BODY:
very light | light | medium | medium-full | full-bodied | heavy

ACIDITY:
tart | crisp | lively | smooth | flabby

TANNINS (IF PRESENT):
LEVEL: low | medium | high   TYPE: soft | round | dry | hard

FLAVOUR INTENSITY:
low | moderate | flavourful | powerful

FLAVOURS:

FINISH:
short (< 3 sec) | medium (4-5) | long (5-7) | v. long (>8 sec)

CONCLUSION/BALANCE:

rating:

FOOD: **FOOD PAIRING:**

                   MATCH: perfect | good | neutral | bad

tasting date: location:

tasting partner(s):

wine name:

producer:

region/appellation:

grape varieties:

vintage: alcohol: price:

COLOUR HUE:
WHITE: greenish | yellow | straw yellow | gold | amber
RED: purple | ruby | red | garnet | brick | brown
ROSÉ: pink | salmon | orange | copper

COLOUR DEPTH:
watery | pale | medium | deep | dark

CLARITY:
clear | slight haze | cloudy

AROMA INTENSITY:
low | moderate | aromatic | powerful

DEVELOPMENT:
youthful | some age | aged

AROMAS:

DRY/SWEET:
bone dry | dry | off dry | medium sweet | sweet | very sweet

BODY:
very light | light | medium | medium-full | full-bodied | heavy

ACIDITY:
tart | crisp | lively | smooth | flabby

TANNINS (IF PRESENT):
LEVEL: low | medium | high   TYPE: soft | round | dry | hard

FLAVOUR INTENSITY:
low | moderate | flavourful | powerful

FLAVOURS:

FINISH:
short (< 3 sec) | medium (4-5) | long (5-7) | v. long (>8 sec)

CONCLUSION/BALANCE:

rating:

FOOD: **FOOD PAIRING:**
                    MATCH: perfect | good | neutral | bad

tasting date: location:

tasting partner(s):

wine name:

producer:

region/appellation:

grape varieties:

vintage: alcohol: price:

COLOUR HUE:
WHITE: greenish | yellow | straw yellow | gold | amber
RED: purple | ruby | red | garnet | brick | brown
ROSÉ: pink | salmon | orange | copper

COLOUR DEPTH:
watery | pale | medium | deep | dark

CLARITY:
clear | slight haze | cloudy

AROMA INTENSITY:
low | moderate | aromatic | powerful

DEVELOPMENT:
youthful | some age | aged

AROMAS:

DRY/SWEET:
bone dry | dry | off dry | medium sweet | sweet | very sweet

BODY:
very light | light | medium | medium-full | full-bodied | heavy

ACIDITY:
tart | crisp | lively | smooth | flabby

TANNINS (IF PRESENT):
LEVEL: low | medium | high   TYPE: soft | round | dry | hard

FLAVOUR INTENSITY:
low | moderate | flavourful | powerful

FLAVOURS:

FINISH:
short (< 3 sec) | medium (4-5) | long (5-7) | v. long (>8 sec)

CONCLUSION/BALANCE:

rating:

FOOD: **FOOD PAIRING:**
                    MATCH: perfect | good | neutral | bad

tasting date: location:

tasting partner(s):

wine name:

producer:

region/appellation:

grape varieties:

vintage: alcohol: price:

COLOUR HUE:

 WHITE: greenish | yellow | straw yellow | gold | amber
RED: purple | ruby | red | garnet | brick | brown
ROSÉ: pink | salmon | orange | copper

COLOUR DEPTH:
watery | pale | medium | deep | dark

CLARITY:
clear | slight haze | cloudy

AROMA INTENSITY:
low | moderate | aromatic | powerful

DEVELOPMENT:
youthful | some age | aged

AROMAS:

DRY/SWEET:
bone dry | dry | off dry | medium sweet | sweet | very sweet

BODY:
very light | light | medium | medium-full | full-bodied | heavy

ACIDITY:
tart | crisp | lively | smooth | flabby

TANNINS (IF PRESENT):
LEVEL: low | medium | high   TYPE: soft | round | dry | hard

FLAVOUR INTENSITY:
low | moderate | flavourful | powerful

FLAVOURS:

FINISH:
short (< 3 sec) | medium (4-5) | long (5-7) | v. long (>8 sec)

CONCLUSION/BALANCE:

rating:

FOOD: **FOOD PAIRING:**

MATCH: perfect | good | neutral | bad

tasting date: location:

tasting partner(s):

wine name:

producer:

region/appellation:

grape varieties:

vintage: alcohol: price:

COLOUR HUE:

WHITE: greenish | yellow | straw yellow | gold | amber
RED: purple | ruby | red | garnet | brick | brown
ROSÉ: pink | salmon | orange | copper

COLOUR DEPTH:
watery | pale | medium | deep | dark

CLARITY:
clear | slight haze | cloudy

AROMA INTENSITY:
low | moderate | aromatic | powerful

DEVELOPMENT:
youthful | some age | aged

AROMAS:

DRY/SWEET:
bone dry | dry | off dry | medium sweet | sweet | very sweet

BODY:
very light | light | medium | medium-full | full-bodied | heavy

ACIDITY:
tart | crisp | lively | smooth | flabby

TANNINS (IF PRESENT):
LEVEL: low | medium | high   TYPE: soft | round | dry | hard

FLAVOUR INTENSITY:
low | moderate | flavourful | powerful

FLAVOURS:

FINISH:
short (< 3 sec) | medium (4-5) | long (5-7) | v. long (>8 sec)

CONCLUSION/BALANCE:

rating:

FOOD: **FOOD PAIRING:**

MATCH: perfect | good | neutral | bad

tasting date: location:

tasting partner(s):

wine name:

producer:

region/appellation:

grape varieties:

vintage: alcohol: price:

COLOUR HUE:

WHITE: greenish | yellow | straw yellow | gold | amber
RED: purple | ruby | red | garnet | brick | brown
ROSÉ: pink | salmon | orange | copper

COLOUR DEPTH:
watery | pale | medium | deep | dark

CLARITY:
clear | slight haze | cloudy

AROMA INTENSITY:
low | moderate | aromatic | powerful

DEVELOPMENT:
youthful | some age | aged

AROMAS:

DRY/SWEET:
bone dry | dry | off dry | medium sweet | sweet | very sweet

BODY:
very light | light | medium | medium-full | full-bodied | heavy

ACIDITY:
tart | crisp | lively | smooth | flabby

TANNINS (IF PRESENT):
LEVEL: low | medium | high   TYPE: soft | round | dry | hard

FLAVOUR INTENSITY:
low | moderate | flavourful | powerful

FLAVOURS:

FINISH:
short (< 3 sec) | medium (4-5) | long (5-7) | v. long (>8 sec)

CONCLUSION/BALANCE:

rating:

FOOD: **FOOD PAIRING:**
MATCH: perfect | good | neutral | bad

tasting date: location:

tasting partner(s):

wine name:

producer:

region/appellation:

grape varieties:

vintage: alcohol: price:

COLOUR HUE:
WHITE: greenish | yellow | straw yellow | gold | amber
RED: purple | ruby | red | garnet | brick | brown
ROSÉ: pink | salmon | orange | copper

COLOUR DEPTH:
watery | pale | medium | deep | dark

CLARITY:
clear | slight haze | cloudy

AROMA INTENSITY:
low | moderate | aromatic | powerful

DEVELOPMENT:
youthful | some age | aged

AROMAS:

DRY/SWEET:
bone dry | dry | off dry | medium sweet | sweet | very sweet

BODY:
very light | light | medium | medium-full | full-bodied | heavy

ACIDITY:
tart | crisp | lively | smooth | flabby

TANNINS (IF PRESENT):
LEVEL: low | medium | high   TYPE: soft | round | dry | hard

FLAVOUR INTENSITY:
low | moderate | flavourful | powerful

FLAVOURS:

FINISH:
short (< 3 sec) | medium (4-5) | long (5-7) | v. long (>8 sec)

CONCLUSION/BALANCE:

rating:

FOOD: **FOOD PAIRING:**
                    MATCH: perfect | good | neutral | bad

tasting date: location:

tasting partner(s):

wine name:

producer:

region/appellation:

grape varieties:

vintage: alcohol: price:

COLOUR HUE:

WHITE: greenish | yellow | straw yellow | gold | amber
RED: purple | ruby | red | garnet | brick | brown
ROSÉ: pink | salmon | orange | copper

COLOUR DEPTH:
watery | pale | medium | deep | dark

CLARITY:
clear | slight haze | cloudy

AROMA INTENSITY:
low | moderate | aromatic | powerful

DEVELOPMENT:
youthful | some age | aged

AROMAS:

DRY/SWEET:
bone dry | dry | off dry | medium sweet | sweet | very sweet

BODY:
very light | light | medium | medium-full | full-bodied | heavy

ACIDITY:
tart | crisp | lively | smooth | flabby

TANNINS (IF PRESENT):
LEVEL: low | medium | high   TYPE: soft | round | dry | hard

FLAVOUR INTENSITY:
low | moderate | flavourful | powerful

FLAVOURS:

FINISH:
short (< 3 sec) | medium (4-5) | long (5-7) | v. long (>8 sec)

CONCLUSION/BALANCE:

rating:

FOOD: **FOOD PAIRING:**

MATCH: perfect | good | neutral | bad

tasting date: location:

tasting partner(s):

wine name:

producer:

region/appellation:

grape varieties:

vintage: alcohol: price:

COLOUR HUE:
WHITE: greenish | yellow | straw yellow | gold | amber
RED: purple | ruby | red | garnet | brick | brown
ROSÉ: pink | salmon | orange | copper

COLOUR DEPTH:
watery | pale | medium | deep | dark

CLARITY:
clear | slight haze | cloudy

AROMA INTENSITY:
low | moderate | aromatic | powerful

DEVELOPMENT:
youthful | some age | aged

AROMAS:

DRY/SWEET:
bone dry | dry | off dry | medium sweet | sweet | very sweet

BODY:
very light | light | medium | medium-full | full-bodied | heavy

ACIDITY:
tart | crisp | lively | smooth | flabby

TANNINS (IF PRESENT):
LEVEL: low | medium | high   TYPE: soft | round | dry | hard

FLAVOUR INTENSITY:
low | moderate | flavourful | powerful

FLAVOURS:

FINISH:
short (< 3 sec) | medium (4-5) | long (5-7) | v. long (>8 sec)

CONCLUSION/BALANCE:

rating:

FOOD: **FOOD PAIRING:**
          MATCH: perfect | good | neutral | bad

tasting date: location:

tasting partner(s):

wine name:

producer:

region/appellation:

grape varieties:

vintage: alcohol: price:

COLOUR HUE:

WHITE: greenish | yellow | straw yellow | gold | amber
RED: purple | ruby | red | garnet | brick | brown
ROSÉ: pink | salmon | orange | copper

COLOUR DEPTH:
watery | pale | medium | deep | dark

CLARITY:
clear | slight haze | cloudy

AROMA INTENSITY:
low | moderate | aromatic | powerful

DEVELOPMENT:
youthful | some age | aged

AROMAS:

DRY/SWEET:
bone dry | dry | off dry | medium sweet | sweet | very sweet

BODY:
very light | light | medium | medium-full | full-bodied | heavy

ACIDITY:
tart | crisp | lively | smooth | flabby

TANNINS (IF PRESENT):
LEVEL: low | medium | high   TYPE: soft | round | dry | hard

FLAVOUR INTENSITY:
low | moderate | flavourful | powerful

FLAVOURS:

FINISH:
short (< 3 sec) | medium (4-5) | long (5-7) | v. long (>8 sec)

CONCLUSION/BALANCE:

rating:

FOOD: **FOOD PAIRING:**

                    MATCH: perfect | good | neutral | bad

tasting date: location:

tasting partner(s):

wine name:

producer:

region/appellation:

grape varieties:

vintage: alcohol: price:

COLOUR HUE:
WHITE: greenish | yellow | straw yellow | gold | amber
RED: purple | ruby | red | garnet | brick | brown
ROSÉ: pink | salmon | orange | copper

COLOUR DEPTH:
watery | pale | medium | deep | dark

CLARITY:
clear | slight haze | cloudy

AROMA INTENSITY:
low | moderate | aromatic | powerful

DEVELOPMENT:
youthful | some age | aged

AROMAS:

DRY/SWEET:
bone dry | dry | off dry | medium sweet | sweet | very sweet

BODY:
very light | light | medium | medium-full | full-bodied | heavy

ACIDITY:
tart | crisp | lively | smooth | flabby

TANNINS (IF PRESENT):
LEVEL: low | medium | high   TYPE: soft | round | dry | hard

FLAVOUR INTENSITY:
low | moderate | flavourful | powerful

FLAVOURS:

FINISH:
short (< 3 sec) | medium (4-5) | long (5-7) | v. long (>8 sec)

CONCLUSION/BALANCE:

rating:

FOOD: **FOOD PAIRING:**
                    MATCH: perfect | good | neutral | bad

tasting date: location:

tasting partner(s):

wine name:

producer:

region/appellation:

grape varieties:

vintage: alcohol: price:

COLOUR HUE:
WHITE: greenish | yellow | straw yellow | gold | amber
RED: purple | ruby | red | garnet | brick | brown
ROSÉ: pink | salmon | orange | copper

COLOUR DEPTH:
watery | pale | medium | deep | dark

CLARITY:
clear | slight haze | cloudy

AROMA INTENSITY:
low | moderate | aromatic | powerful

DEVELOPMENT:
youthful | some age | aged

AROMAS:

DRY/SWEET:
bone dry | dry | off dry | medium sweet | sweet | very sweet

BODY:
very light | light | medium | medium-full | full-bodied | heavy

ACIDITY:
tart | crisp | lively | smooth | flabby

TANNINS (IF PRESENT):
LEVEL: low | medium | high   TYPE: soft | round | dry | hard

FLAVOUR INTENSITY:
low | moderate | flavourful | powerful

FLAVOURS:

FINISH:
short (< 3 sec) | medium (4-5) | long (5-7) | v. long (>8 sec)

CONCLUSION/BALANCE:

rating:

FOOD: **FOOD PAIRING:**
                 MATCH: perfect | good | neutral | bad

tasting date: location:

tasting partner(s):

wine name:

producer:

region/appellation:

grape varieties:

vintage: alcohol: price:

COLOUR HUE:

WHITE: greenish | yellow | straw yellow | gold | amber
RED: purple | ruby | red | garnet | brick | brown
ROSÉ: pink | salmon | orange | copper

COLOUR DEPTH:
watery | pale | medium | deep | dark

CLARITY:
clear | slight haze | cloudy

AROMA INTENSITY:
low | moderate | aromatic | powerful

DEVELOPMENT:
youthful | some age | aged

AROMAS:

DRY/SWEET:
bone dry | dry | off dry | medium sweet | sweet | very sweet

BODY:
very light | light | medium | medium-full | full-bodied | heavy

ACIDITY:
tart | crisp | lively | smooth | flabby

TANNINS (IF PRESENT):
LEVEL: low | medium | high   TYPE: soft | round | dry | hard

FLAVOUR INTENSITY:
low | moderate | flavourful | powerful

FLAVOURS:

FINISH:
short (< 3 sec) | medium (4-5) | long (5-7) | v. long (>8 sec)

CONCLUSION/BALANCE:

rating:

FOOD: **FOOD PAIRING:**

MATCH: perfect | good | neutral | bad

tasting date: location:

tasting partner(s):

wine name:

producer:

region/appellation:

grape varieties:

vintage: alcohol: price:

COLOUR HUE:

WHITE: greenish | yellow | straw yellow | gold | amber
RED: purple | ruby | red | garnet | brick | brown
ROSÉ: pink | salmon | orange | copper

COLOUR DEPTH:
watery | pale | medium | deep | dark

CLARITY:
clear | slight haze | cloudy

AROMA INTENSITY:
low | moderate | aromatic | powerful

DEVELOPMENT:
youthful | some age | aged

AROMAS:

DRY/SWEET:
bone dry | dry | off dry | medium sweet | sweet | very sweet

BODY:
very light | light | medium | medium-full | full-bodied | heavy

ACIDITY:
tart | crisp | lively | smooth | flabby

TANNINS (IF PRESENT):
LEVEL: low | medium | high   TYPE: soft | round | dry | hard

FLAVOUR INTENSITY:
low | moderate | flavourful | powerful

FLAVOURS:

FINISH:
short (< 3 sec) | medium (4-5) | long (5-7) | v. long (>8 sec)

CONCLUSION/BALANCE:

rating:

FOOD: **FOOD PAIRING:**
                    MATCH: perfect | good | neutral | bad

tasting date: location:

tasting partner(s):

wine name:

producer:

region/appellation:

grape varieties:

vintage: alcohol: price:

COLOUR HUE:

WHITE: greenish | yellow | straw yellow | gold | amber
RED: purple | ruby | red | garnet | brick | brown
ROSÉ: pink | salmon | orange | copper

COLOUR DEPTH:
watery | pale | medium | deep | dark

CLARITY:
clear | slight haze | cloudy

AROMA INTENSITY:
low | moderate | aromatic | powerful

DEVELOPMENT:
youthful | some age | aged

AROMAS:

DRY/SWEET:
bone dry | dry | off dry | medium sweet | sweet | very sweet

BODY:
very light | light | medium | medium-full | full-bodied | heavy

ACIDITY:
tart | crisp | lively | smooth | flabby

TANNINS (IF PRESENT):
LEVEL: low | medium | high   TYPE: soft | round | dry | hard

FLAVOUR INTENSITY:
low | moderate | flavourful | powerful

FLAVOURS:

FINISH:
short (< 3 sec) | medium (4-5) | long (5-7) | v. long (>8 sec)

CONCLUSION/BALANCE:

rating:

FOOD: **FOOD PAIRING:**

MATCH: perfect | good | neutral | bad

tasting date: location:

tasting partner(s):

wine name:

producer:

region/appellation:

grape varieties:

vintage: alcohol: price:

COLOUR HUE:
WHITE: greenish | yellow | straw yellow | gold | amber
RED: purple | ruby | red | garnet | brick | brown
ROSÉ: pink | salmon | orange | copper

COLOUR DEPTH:
watery | pale | medium | deep | dark

CLARITY:
clear | slight haze | cloudy

AROMA INTENSITY:
low | moderate | aromatic | powerful

DEVELOPMENT:
youthful | some age | aged

AROMAS:

DRY/SWEET:
bone dry | dry | off dry | medium sweet | sweet | very sweet

BODY:
very light | light | medium | medium-full | full-bodied | heavy

ACIDITY:
tart | crisp | lively | smooth | flabby

TANNINS (IF PRESENT):
LEVEL: low | medium | high   TYPE: soft | round | dry | hard

FLAVOUR INTENSITY:
low | moderate | flavourful | powerful

FLAVOURS:

FINISH:
short (< 3 sec) | medium (4-5) | long (5-7) | v. long (>8 sec)

CONCLUSION/BALANCE:

rating:

FOOD: **FOOD PAIRING:**
                         MATCH: perfect | good | neutral | bad

tasting date: location:

tasting partner(s):

wine name:

producer:

region/appellation:

grape varieties:

vintage: alcohol: price:

COLOUR HUE:

WHITE: greenish | yellow | straw yellow | gold | amber
RED: purple | ruby | red | garnet | brick | brown
ROSÉ: pink | salmon | orange | copper

COLOUR DEPTH:
watery | pale | medium | deep | dark

CLARITY:
clear | slight haze | cloudy

AROMA INTENSITY:
low | moderate | aromatic | powerful

DEVELOPMENT:
youthful | some age | aged

AROMAS:

DRY/SWEET:
bone dry | dry | off dry | medium sweet | sweet | very sweet

BODY:
very light | light | medium | medium-full | full-bodied | heavy

ACIDITY:
tart | crisp | lively | smooth | flabby

TANNINS (IF PRESENT):
LEVEL: low | medium | high   TYPE: soft | round | dry | hard

FLAVOUR INTENSITY:
low | moderate | flavourful | powerful

FLAVOURS:

FINISH:
short (< 3 sec) | medium (4-5) | long (5-7) | v. long (>8 sec)

CONCLUSION/BALANCE:

rating:

FOOD: **FOOD PAIRING:**

MATCH: perfect | good | neutral | bad

tasting date: location:

tasting partner(s):

wine name:

producer:

region/appellation:

grape varieties:

vintage: alcohol: price:

COLOUR HUE:

WHITE: greenish | yellow | straw yellow | gold | amber
RED: purple | ruby | red | garnet | brick | brown
ROSÉ: pink | salmon | orange | copper

COLOUR DEPTH:
watery | pale | medium | deep | dark

CLARITY:
clear | slight haze | cloudy

AROMA INTENSITY:
low | moderate | aromatic | powerful

DEVELOPMENT:
youthful | some age | aged

AROMAS:

DRY/SWEET:
bone dry | dry | off dry | medium sweet | sweet | very sweet

BODY:
very light | light | medium | medium-full | full-bodied | heavy

ACIDITY:
tart | crisp | lively | smooth | flabby

TANNINS (IF PRESENT):
LEVEL: low | medium | high   TYPE: soft | round | dry | hard

FLAVOUR INTENSITY:
low | moderate | flavourful | powerful

FLAVOURS:

FINISH:
short (< 3 sec) | medium (4-5) | long (5-7) | v. long (>8 sec)

CONCLUSION/BALANCE:

rating:

FOOD: **FOOD PAIRING:**

MATCH: perfect | good | neutral | bad

tasting date: location:

tasting partner(s):

wine name:

producer:

region/appellation:

grape varieties:

vintage: alcohol: price:

COLOUR HUE:

WHITE: greenish | yellow | straw yellow | gold | amber
RED: purple | ruby | red | garnet | brick | brown
ROSÉ: pink | salmon | orange | copper

COLOUR DEPTH:
watery | pale | medium | deep | dark

CLARITY:
clear | slight haze | cloudy

AROMA INTENSITY:
low | moderate | aromatic | powerful

DEVELOPMENT:
youthful | some age | aged

AROMAS:

DRY/SWEET:
bone dry | dry | off dry | medium sweet | sweet | very sweet

BODY:
very light | light | medium | medium-full | full-bodied | heavy

ACIDITY:
tart | crisp | lively | smooth | flabby

TANNINS (IF PRESENT):
LEVEL: low | medium | high   TYPE: soft | round | dry | hard

FLAVOUR INTENSITY:
low | moderate | flavourful | powerful

FLAVOURS:

FINISH:
short (< 3 sec) | medium (4-5) | long (5-7) | v. long (>8 sec)

CONCLUSION/BALANCE:

rating:

FOOD: **FOOD PAIRING:**

MATCH: perfect | good | neutral | bad

tasting date: location:

tasting partner(s):

wine name:

producer:

region/appellation:

grape varieties:

vintage: alcohol: price:

COLOUR HUE:
WHITE: greenish | yellow | straw yellow | gold | amber
RED: purple | ruby | red | garnet | brick | brown
ROSÉ: pink | salmon | orange | copper

COLOUR DEPTH:
watery | pale | medium | deep | dark

CLARITY:
clear | slight haze | cloudy

AROMA INTENSITY:
low | moderate | aromatic | powerful

DEVELOPMENT:
youthful | some age | aged

AROMAS:

DRY/SWEET:
bone dry | dry | off dry | medium sweet | sweet | very sweet

BODY:
very light | light | medium | medium-full | full-bodied | heavy

ACIDITY:
tart | crisp | lively | smooth | flabby

TANNINS (IF PRESENT):
LEVEL: low | medium | high   TYPE: soft | round | dry | hard

FLAVOUR INTENSITY:
low | moderate | flavourful | powerful

FLAVOURS: ˙

FINISH:
short (< 3 sec) | medium (4-5) | long (5-7) | v. long (>8 sec)

CONCLUSION/BALANCE:

rating:

FOOD: **FOOD PAIRING:**
                   MATCH: perfect | good | neutral | bad

tasting date: location:

tasting partner(s):

wine name:

producer:

region/appellation:

grape varieties:

vintage: alcohol: price:

COLOUR HUE:

WHITE: greenish | yellow | straw yellow | gold | amber
RED: purple | ruby | red | garnet | brick | brown
ROSÉ: pink | salmon | orange | copper

COLOUR DEPTH:
watery | pale | medium | deep | dark

CLARITY:
clear | slight haze | cloudy

AROMA INTENSITY:

low | moderate | aromatic | powerful

DEVELOPMENT:
youthful | some age | aged

AROMAS:

DRY/SWEET:
bone dry | dry | off dry | medium sweet | sweet | very sweet

BODY:
very light | light | medium | medium-full | full-bodied | heavy

ACIDITY:
tart | crisp | lively | smooth | flabby

TANNINS (IF PRESENT):
LEVEL: low | medium | high   TYPE: soft | round | dry | hard

FLAVOUR INTENSITY:
low | moderate | flavourful | powerful

FLAVOURS:

FINISH:
short (< 3 sec) | medium (4-5) | long (5-7) | v. long (>8 sec)

CONCLUSION/BALANCE:

rating:

FOOD: **FOOD PAIRING:**

MATCH: perfect | good | neutral | bad

tasting date: location:

tasting partner(s):

wine name:

producer:

region/appellation:

grape varieties:

vintage: alcohol: price:

COLOUR HUE:

WHITE: greenish | yellow | straw yellow | gold | amber
RED: purple | ruby | red | garnet | brick | brown
ROSÉ: pink | salmon | orange | copper

COLOUR DEPTH:
watery | pale | medium | deep | dark

CLARITY:
clear | slight haze | cloudy

AROMA INTENSITY:
low | moderate | aromatic | powerful

DEVELOPMENT:
youthful | some age | aged

AROMAS:

DRY/SWEET:
bone dry | dry | off dry | medium sweet | sweet | very sweet

BODY:
very light | light | medium | medium-full | full-bodied | heavy

ACIDITY:
tart | crisp | lively | smooth | flabby

TANNINS (IF PRESENT):
LEVEL: low | medium | high   TYPE: soft | round | dry | hard

FLAVOUR INTENSITY:
low | moderate | flavourful | powerful

FLAVOURS:

FINISH:
short (< 3 sec) | medium (4-5) | long (5-7) | v. long (>8 sec)

CONCLUSION/BALANCE:

rating:

FOOD: **FOOD PAIRING:**

MATCH: perfect | good | neutral | bad

tasting date: location:

tasting partner(s):

wine name:

producer:

region/appellation:

grape varieties:

vintage: alcohol: price:

COLOUR HUE:
WHITE: greenish | yellow | straw yellow | gold | amber
RED: purple | ruby | red | garnet | brick | brown
ROSÉ: pink | salmon | orange | copper
COLOUR DEPTH:
watery | pale | medium | deep | dark
CLARITY:
clear | slight haze | cloudy

AROMA INTENSITY:
low | moderate | aromatic | powerful
DEVELOPMENT:
youthful | some age | aged
AROMAS:

DRY/SWEET:
bone dry | dry | off dry | medium sweet | sweet | very sweet
BODY:
very light | light | medium | medium-full | full-bodied | heavy
ACIDITY:
tart | crisp | lively | smooth | flabby
TANNINS (IF PRESENT):
LEVEL: low | medium | high   TYPE: soft | round | dry | hard
FLAVOUR INTENSITY:
low | moderate | flavourful | powerful
FLAVOURS:

FINISH:
short (< 3 sec) | medium (4-5) | long (5-7) | v. long (>8 sec)

CONCLUSION/BALANCE:

rating:

FOOD: **FOOD PAIRING:**
                   MATCH: perfect | good | neutral | bad

tasting date: location:

tasting partner(s):

wine name:

producer:

region/appellation:

grape varieties:

vintage: alcohol: price:

COLOUR HUE:

WHITE: greenish | yellow | straw yellow | gold | amber
RED: purple | ruby | red | garnet | brick | brown
ROSÉ: pink | salmon | orange | copper

COLOUR DEPTH:
watery | pale | medium | deep | dark

CLARITY:
clear | slight haze | cloudy

AROMA INTENSITY:
low | moderate | aromatic | powerful

DEVELOPMENT:
youthful | some age | aged

AROMAS:

DRY/SWEET:
bone dry | dry | off dry | medium sweet | sweet | very sweet

BODY:
very light | light | medium | medium-full | full-bodied | heavy

ACIDITY:
tart | crisp | lively | smooth | flabby

TANNINS (IF PRESENT):
LEVEL: low | medium | high   TYPE: soft | round | dry | hard

FLAVOUR INTENSITY:
low | moderate | flavourful | powerful

FLAVOURS:

FINISH:
short (< 3 sec) | medium (4-5) | long (5-7) | v. long (>8 sec)

CONCLUSION/BALANCE:

rating:

FOOD: **FOOD PAIRING:**
                  MATCH: perfect | good | neutral | bad

tasting date: location:

tasting partner(s):

wine name:

producer:

region/appellation:

grape varieties:

vintage: alcohol: price:

COLOUR HUE:
WHITE: greenish | yellow | straw yellow | gold | amber
RED: purple | ruby | red | garnet | brick | brown
ROSÉ: pink | salmon | orange | copper

COLOUR DEPTH:
watery | pale | medium | deep | dark

CLARITY:
clear | slight haze | cloudy

AROMA INTENSITY:
low | moderate | aromatic | powerful

DEVELOPMENT:
youthful | some age | aged

AROMAS:

DRY/SWEET:
bone dry | dry | off dry | medium sweet | sweet | very sweet

BODY:
very light | light | medium | medium-full | full-bodied | heavy

ACIDITY:
tart | crisp | lively | smooth | flabby

TANNINS (IF PRESENT):
LEVEL: low | medium | high   TYPE: soft | round | dry | hard

FLAVOUR INTENSITY:
low | moderate | flavourful | powerful

FLAVOURS:

FINISH:
short (< 3 sec) | medium (4-5) | long (5-7) | v. long (>8 sec)

CONCLUSION/BALANCE:

rating:

FOOD: **FOOD PAIRING:**

MATCH: perfect | good | neutral | bad

tasting date: location:

tasting partner(s):

wine name:

producer:

region/appellation:

grape varieties:

vintage: alcohol: price:

COLOUR HUE:
WHITE: greenish | yellow | straw yellow | gold | amber
RED: purple | ruby | red | garnet | brick | brown
ROSÉ: pink | salmon | orange | copper

COLOUR DEPTH:
watery | pale | medium | deep | dark

CLARITY:
clear | slight haze | cloudy

AROMA INTENSITY:
low | moderate | aromatic | powerful

DEVELOPMENT:
youthful | some age | aged

AROMAS:

DRY/SWEET:
bone dry | dry | off dry | medium sweet | sweet | very sweet

BODY:
very light | light | medium | medium-full | full-bodied | heavy

ACIDITY:
tart | crisp | lively | smooth | flabby

TANNINS (IF PRESENT):
LEVEL: low | medium | high   TYPE: soft | round | dry | hard

FLAVOUR INTENSITY:
low | moderate | flavourful | powerful

FLAVOURS:

FINISH:
short (< 3 sec) | medium (4-5) | long (5-7) | v. long (>8 sec)

CONCLUSION/BALANCE:

rating:

FOOD: **FOOD PAIRING:**
                   MATCH: perfect | good | neutral | bad

tasting date: location:

tasting partner(s):

wine name:

producer:

region/appellation:

grape varieties:

vintage: alcohol: price:

COLOUR HUE:
WHITE: greenish | yellow | straw yellow | gold | amber
RED: purple | ruby | red | garnet | brick | brown
ROSÉ: pink | salmon | orange | copper

COLOUR DEPTH:
watery | pale | medium | deep | dark

CLARITY:
clear | slight haze | cloudy

AROMA INTENSITY:
low | moderate | aromatic | powerful

DEVELOPMENT:
youthful | some age | aged

AROMAS:

DRY/SWEET:
bone dry | dry | off dry | medium sweet | sweet | very sweet

BODY:
very light | light | medium | medium-full | full-bodied | heavy

ACIDITY:
tart | crisp | lively | smooth | flabby

TANNINS (IF PRESENT):
LEVEL: low | medium | high   TYPE: soft | round | dry | hard

FLAVOUR INTENSITY:
low | moderate | flavourful | powerful

FLAVOURS:

FINISH:
short (< 3 sec) | medium (4-5) | long (5-7) | v. long (>8 sec)

CONCLUSION/BALANCE:

rating:

FOOD: **FOOD PAIRING:**

MATCH: perfect | good | neutral | bad

tasting date: location:

tasting partner(s):

wine name:

producer:

region/appellation:

grape varieties:

vintage: alcohol: price:

COLOUR HUE:

WHITE: greenish | yellow | straw yellow | gold | amber
RED: purple | ruby | red | garnet | brick | brown
ROSÉ: pink | salmon | orange | copper

COLOUR DEPTH:
watery | pale | medium | deep | dark

CLARITY:
clear | slight haze | cloudy

AROMA INTENSITY:
low | moderate | aromatic | powerful

DEVELOPMENT:
youthful | some age | aged

AROMAS:

DRY/SWEET:
bone dry | dry | off dry | medium sweet | sweet | very sweet

BODY:
very light | light | medium | medium-full | full-bodied | heavy

ACIDITY:
tart | crisp | lively | smooth | flabby

TANNINS (IF PRESENT):
LEVEL: low | medium | high   TYPE: soft | round | dry | hard

FLAVOUR INTENSITY:
low | moderate | flavourful | powerful

FLAVOURS:

FINISH:
short (< 3 sec) | medium (4-5) | long (5-7) | v. long (>8 sec)

CONCLUSION/BALANCE:

rating:

FOOD: **FOOD PAIRING:**
                MATCH: perfect | good | neutral | bad

tasting date: location:

tasting partner(s):

wine name:

producer:

region/appellation:

grape varieties:

vintage: alcohol: price:

COLOUR HUE:
WHITE: greenish | yellow | straw yellow | gold | amber
RED: purple | ruby | red | garnet | brick | brown
ROSÉ: pink | salmon | orange | copper

COLOUR DEPTH:
watery | pale | medium | deep | dark

CLARITY:
clear | slight haze | cloudy

AROMA INTENSITY:
low | moderate | aromatic | powerful

DEVELOPMENT:
youthful | some age | aged

AROMAS:

DRY/SWEET:
bone dry | dry | off dry | medium sweet | sweet | very sweet

BODY:
very light | light | medium | medium-full | full-bodied | heavy

ACIDITY:
tart | crisp | lively | smooth | flabby

TANNINS (IF PRESENT):
LEVEL: low | medium | high   TYPE: soft | round | dry | hard

FLAVOUR INTENSITY:
low | moderate | flavourful | powerful

FLAVOURS:

FINISH:
short (< 3 sec) | medium (4-5) | long (5-7) | v. long (>8 sec)

CONCLUSION/BALANCE:

rating:

FOOD: **FOOD PAIRING:**
                         MATCH: perfect | good | neutral | bad

tasting date: location:

tasting partner(s):

wine name:

producer:

region/appellation:

grape varieties:

vintage: alcohol: price:

COLOUR HUE:

WHITE: greenish | yellow | straw yellow | gold | amber
RED: purple | ruby | red | garnet | brick | brown
ROSÉ: pink | salmon | orange | copper

COLOUR DEPTH:
watery | pale | medium | deep | dark

CLARITY:
clear | slight haze | cloudy

AROMA INTENSITY:
low | moderate | aromatic | powerful

DEVELOPMENT:
youthful | some age | aged

AROMAS:

DRY/SWEET:
bone dry | dry | off dry | medium sweet | sweet | very sweet

BODY:
very light | light | medium | medium-full | full-bodied | heavy

ACIDITY:
tart | crisp | lively | smooth | flabby

TANNINS (IF PRESENT):
LEVEL: low | medium | high   TYPE: soft | round | dry | hard

FLAVOUR INTENSITY:
low | moderate | flavourful | powerful

FLAVOURS:

FINISH:
short (< 3 sec) | medium (4-5) | long (5-7) | v. long (>8 sec)

CONCLUSION/BALANCE:

rating:

FOOD: **FOOD PAIRING:**

MATCH: perfect | good | neutral | bad

tasting date: location:

tasting partner(s):

wine name:

producer:

region/appellation:

grape varieties:

vintage: alcohol: price:

COLOUR HUE:
WHITE: greenish | yellow | straw yellow | gold | amber
RED: purple | ruby | red | garnet | brick | brown
ROSÉ: pink | salmon | orange | copper

COLOUR DEPTH:
watery | pale | medium | deep | dark

CLARITY:
clear | slight haze | cloudy

AROMA INTENSITY:
low | moderate | aromatic | powerful

DEVELOPMENT:
youthful | some age | aged

AROMAS:

DRY/SWEET:
bone dry | dry | off dry | medium sweet | sweet | very sweet

BODY:
very light | light | medium | medium-full | full-bodied | heavy

ACIDITY:
tart | crisp | lively | smooth | flabby

TANNINS (IF PRESENT):
LEVEL: low | medium | high   TYPE: soft | round | dry | hard

FLAVOUR INTENSITY:
low | moderate | flavourful | powerful

FLAVOURS:

FINISH:
short (< 3 sec) | medium (4-5) | long (5-7) | v. long (>8 sec)

CONCLUSION/BALANCE:

rating:

FOOD: **FOOD PAIRING:**

                    MATCH: perfect | good | neutral | bad

tasting date: location:

tasting partner(s):

wine name:

producer:

region/appellation:

grape varieties:

vintage: alcohol: price:

COLOUR HUE:
WHITE: greenish | yellow | straw yellow | gold | amber
RED: purple | ruby | red | garnet | brick | brown
ROSÉ: pink | salmon | orange | copper

COLOUR DEPTH:
watery | pale | medium | deep | dark

CLARITY:
clear | slight haze | cloudy

AROMA INTENSITY:
low | moderate | aromatic | powerful

DEVELOPMENT:
youthful | some age | aged

AROMAS:

DRY/SWEET:
bone dry | dry | off dry | medium sweet | sweet | very sweet

BODY:
very light | light | medium | medium-full | full-bodied | heavy

ACIDITY:
tart | crisp | lively | smooth | flabby

TANNINS (IF PRESENT):
LEVEL: low | medium | high   TYPE: soft | round | dry | hard

FLAVOUR INTENSITY:
low | moderate | flavourful | powerful

FLAVOURS:

FINISH:
short (< 3 sec) | medium (4-5) | long (5-7) | v. long (>8 sec)

CONCLUSION/BALANCE:

rating:

FOOD: **FOOD PAIRING:**
                       MATCH: perfect | good | neutral | bad

tasting date: location:

tasting partner(s):

wine name:

producer:

region/appellation:

grape varieties:

vintage: alcohol: price:

COLOUR HUE:

WHITE: greenish | yellow | straw yellow | gold | amber
RED: purple | ruby | red | garnet | brick | brown
ROSÉ: pink | salmon | orange | copper

COLOUR DEPTH:
watery | pale | medium | deep | dark

CLARITY:
clear | slight haze | cloudy

AROMA INTENSITY:
low | moderate | aromatic | powerful

DEVELOPMENT:
youthful | some age | aged

AROMAS:

DRY/SWEET:
bone dry | dry | off dry | medium sweet | sweet | very sweet

BODY:
very light | light | medium | medium-full | full-bodied | heavy

ACIDITY:
tart | crisp | lively | smooth | flabby

TANNINS (IF PRESENT):
LEVEL: low | medium | high   TYPE: soft | round | dry | hard

FLAVOUR INTENSITY:
low | moderate | flavourful | powerful

FLAVOURS:

FINISH:
short (< 3 sec) | medium (4-5) | long (5-7) | v. long (>8 sec)

CONCLUSION/BALANCE:

rating:

FOOD: **FOOD PAIRING:**

MATCH: perfect | good | neutral | bad

tasting date: location:

tasting partner(s):

wine name:

producer:

region/appellation:

grape varieties:

vintage: alcohol: price:

COLOUR HUE:
WHITE: greenish | yellow | straw yellow | gold | amber
RED: purple | ruby | red | garnet | brick | brown
ROSÉ: pink | salmon | orange | copper

COLOUR DEPTH:
watery | pale | medium | deep | dark

CLARITY:
clear | slight haze | cloudy

AROMA INTENSITY:
low | moderate | aromatic | powerful

DEVELOPMENT:
youthful | some age | aged

AROMAS:

DRY/SWEET:
bone dry | dry | off dry | medium sweet | sweet | very sweet

BODY:
very light | light | medium | medium-full | full-bodied | heavy

ACIDITY:
tart | crisp | lively | smooth | flabby

TANNINS (IF PRESENT):
LEVEL: low | medium | high   TYPE: soft | round | dry | hard

FLAVOUR INTENSITY:
low | moderate | flavourful | powerful

FLAVOURS:

FINISH:
short (< 3 sec) | medium (4-5) | long (5-7) | v. long (>8 sec)

CONCLUSION/BALANCE:

rating:

FOOD: **FOOD PAIRING:**

MATCH: perfect | good | neutral | bad

tasting date: location:

tasting partner(s):

wine name:

producer:

region/appellation:

grape varieties:

vintage: alcohol: price:

COLOUR HUE:
WHITE: greenish | yellow | straw yellow | gold | amber
RED: purple | ruby | red | garnet | brick | brown
ROSÉ: pink | salmon | orange | copper

COLOUR DEPTH:
watery | pale | medium | deep | dark

CLARITY:
clear | slight haze | cloudy

AROMA INTENSITY:
low | moderate | aromatic | powerful

DEVELOPMENT:
youthful | some age | aged

AROMAS:

DRY/SWEET:
bone dry | dry | off dry | medium sweet | sweet | very sweet

BODY:
very light | light | medium | medium-full | full-bodied | heavy

ACIDITY:
tart | crisp | lively | smooth | flabby

TANNINS (IF PRESENT):
LEVEL: low | medium | high   TYPE: soft | round | dry | hard

FLAVOUR INTENSITY:
low | moderate | flavourful | powerful

FLAVOURS:

FINISH:
short (< 3 sec) | medium (4-5) | long (5-7) | v. long (>8 sec)

CONCLUSION/BALANCE:

rating:

FOOD: **FOOD PAIRING:**
                    MATCH: perfect | good | neutral | bad

tasting date: location:

tasting partner(s):

wine name:

producer:

region/appellation:

grape varieties:

vintage: alcohol: price:

COLOUR HUE:

WHITE: greenish | yellow | straw yellow | gold | amber
RED: purple | ruby | red | garnet | brick | brown
ROSÉ: pink | salmon | orange | copper

COLOUR DEPTH:
watery | pale | medium | deep | dark

CLARITY:
clear | slight haze | cloudy

AROMA INTENSITY:
low | moderate | aromatic | powerful

DEVELOPMENT:
youthful | some age | aged

AROMAS:

DRY/SWEET:
bone dry | dry | off dry | medium sweet | sweet | very sweet

BODY:
very light | light | medium | medium-full | full-bodied | heavy

ACIDITY:
tart | crisp | lively | smooth | flabby

TANNINS (IF PRESENT):
LEVEL: low | medium | high   TYPE: soft | round | dry | hard

FLAVOUR INTENSITY:
low | moderate | flavourful | powerful

FLAVOURS:

FINISH:
short (< 3 sec) | medium (4-5) | long (5-7) | v. long (>8 sec)

CONCLUSION/BALANCE:

rating:

FOOD: **FOOD PAIRING:**

MATCH: perfect | good | neutral | bad

tasting date: location:

tasting partner(s):

wine name:

producer:

region/appellation:

grape varieties:

vintage: alcohol: price:

COLOUR HUE:
WHITE: greenish | yellow | straw yellow | gold | amber
RED: purple | ruby | red | garnet | brick | brown
ROSÉ: pink | salmon | orange | copper

COLOUR DEPTH:
watery | pale | medium | deep | dark

CLARITY:
clear | slight haze | cloudy

AROMA INTENSITY:
low | moderate | aromatic | powerful

DEVELOPMENT:
youthful | some age | aged

AROMAS:

DRY/SWEET:
bone dry | dry | off dry | medium sweet | sweet | very sweet

BODY:
very light | light | medium | medium-full | full-bodied | heavy

ACIDITY:
tart | crisp | lively | smooth | flabby

TANNINS (IF PRESENT):
LEVEL: low | medium | high   TYPE: soft | round | dry | hard

FLAVOUR INTENSITY:
low | moderate | flavourful | powerful

FLAVOURS:

FINISH:
short (< 3 sec) | medium (4-5) | long (5-7) | v. long (>8 sec)

CONCLUSION/BALANCE:

rating:

FOOD: **FOOD PAIRING:**

MATCH: perfect | good | neutral | bad

tasting date: location:

tasting partner(s):

wine name:

producer:

region/appellation:

grape varieties:

vintage: alcohol: price:

COLOUR HUE:

WHITE: greenish | yellow | straw yellow | gold | amber
RED: purple | ruby | red | garnet | brick | brown
ROSÉ: pink | salmon | orange | copper

COLOUR DEPTH:
watery | pale | medium | deep | dark

CLARITY:
clear | slight haze | cloudy

AROMA INTENSITY:
low | moderate | aromatic | powerful

DEVELOPMENT:
youthful | some age | aged

AROMAS:

DRY/SWEET:
bone dry | dry | off dry | medium sweet | sweet | very sweet

BODY:
very light | light | medium | medium-full | full-bodied | heavy

ACIDITY:
tart | crisp | lively | smooth | flabby

TANNINS (IF PRESENT):
LEVEL: low | medium | high   TYPE: soft | round | dry | hard

FLAVOUR INTENSITY:
low | moderate | flavourful | powerful

FLAVOURS:

FINISH:
short (< 3 sec) | medium (4-5) | long (5-7) | v. long (>8 sec)

CONCLUSION/BALANCE:

rating:

FOOD: **FOOD PAIRING:**

MATCH: perfect | good | neutral | bad

tasting date: location:

tasting partner(s):

wine name:

producer:

region/appellation:

grape varieties:

vintage: alcohol: price:

COLOUR HUE:
WHITE: greenish | yellow | straw yellow | gold | amber
RED: purple | ruby | red | garnet | brick | brown
ROSÉ: pink | salmon | orange | copper

COLOUR DEPTH:
watery | pale | medium | deep | dark

CLARITY:
clear | slight haze | cloudy

AROMA INTENSITY:
low | moderate | aromatic | powerful

DEVELOPMENT:
youthful | some age | aged

AROMAS:

DRY/SWEET:
bone dry | dry | off dry | medium sweet | sweet | very sweet

BODY:
very light | light | medium | medium-full | full-bodied | heavy

ACIDITY:
tart | crisp | lively | smooth | flabby

TANNINS (IF PRESENT):
LEVEL: low | medium | high   TYPE: soft | round | dry | hard

FLAVOUR INTENSITY:
low | moderate | flavourful | powerful

FLAVOURS:

FINISH:
short (< 3 sec) | medium (4-5) | long (5-7) | v. long (>8 sec)

CONCLUSION/BALANCE:

rating:

FOOD: **FOOD PAIRING:**
               MATCH: perfect | good | neutral | bad

tasting date: location:

tasting partner(s):

wine name:

producer:

region/appellation:

grape varieties:

vintage: alcohol: price:

COLOUR HUE:

WHITE: greenish | yellow | straw yellow | gold | amber
RED: purple | ruby | red | garnet | brick | brown
ROSÉ: pink | salmon | orange | copper
COLOUR DEPTH:
watery | pale | medium | deep | dark
CLARITY:
clear | slight haze | cloudy

AROMA INTENSITY:
low | moderate | aromatic | powerful
DEVELOPMENT:
youthful | some age | aged
AROMAS:

DRY/SWEET:
bone dry | dry | off dry | medium sweet | sweet | very sweet
BODY:
very light | light | medium | medium-full | full-bodied | heavy
ACIDITY:
tart | crisp | lively | smooth | flabby
TANNINS (IF PRESENT):
LEVEL: low | medium | high   TYPE: soft | round | dry | hard
FLAVOUR INTENSITY:
low | moderate | flavourful | powerful
FLAVOURS:

FINISH:
short (< 3 sec) | medium (4-5) | long (5-7) | v. long (>8 sec)

CONCLUSION/BALANCE:

rating:

FOOD: **FOOD PAIRING:**
                MATCH: perfect | good | neutral | bad

tasting date: location:

tasting partner(s):

wine name:

producer:

region/appellation:

grape varieties:

vintage: alcohol: price:

COLOUR HUE:
WHITE: greenish | yellow | straw yellow | gold | amber
RED: purple | ruby | red | garnet | brick | brown
ROSÉ: pink | salmon | orange | copper

COLOUR DEPTH:
watery | pale | medium | deep | dark

CLARITY:
clear | slight haze | cloudy

AROMA INTENSITY:
low | moderate | aromatic | powerful

DEVELOPMENT:
youthful | some age | aged

AROMAS:

DRY/SWEET:
bone dry | dry | off dry | medium sweet | sweet | very sweet

BODY:
very light | light | medium | medium-full | full-bodied | heavy

ACIDITY:
tart | crisp | lively | smooth | flabby

TANNINS (IF PRESENT):
LEVEL: low | medium | high   TYPE: soft | round | dry | hard

FLAVOUR INTENSITY:
low | moderate | flavourful | powerful

FLAVOURS:

FINISH:
short (< 3 sec) | medium (4-5) | long (5-7) | v. long (>8 sec)

CONCLUSION/BALANCE:

rating:

FOOD: **FOOD PAIRING:**
                MATCH: perfect | good | neutral | bad

tasting date: location:

tasting partner(s):

wine name:

producer:

region/appellation:

grape varieties:

vintage: alcohol: price:

COLOUR HUE:
WHITE: greenish | yellow | straw yellow | gold | amber
RED: purple | ruby | red | garnet | brick | brown
ROSÉ: pink | salmon | orange | copper

COLOUR DEPTH:
watery | pale | medium | deep | dark

CLARITY:
clear | slight haze | cloudy

AROMA INTENSITY:
low | moderate | aromatic | powerful

DEVELOPMENT:
youthful | some age | aged

AROMAS:

DRY/SWEET:
bone dry | dry | off dry | medium sweet | sweet | very sweet

BODY:
very light | light | medium | medium-full | full-bodied | heavy

ACIDITY:
tart | crisp | lively | smooth | flabby

TANNINS (IF PRESENT):
LEVEL: low | medium | high   TYPE: soft | round | dry | hard

FLAVOUR INTENSITY:
low | moderate | flavourful | powerful

FLAVOURS:

FINISH:
short (< 3 sec) | medium (4-5) | long (5-7) | v. long (>8 sec)

CONCLUSION/BALANCE:

rating:

FOOD: **FOOD PAIRING:**
MATCH: perfect | good | neutral | bad

tasting date: location:

tasting partner(s):

wine name:

producer:

region/appellation:

grape varieties:

vintage: alcohol: price:

COLOUR HUE:
WHITE: greenish | yellow | straw yellow | gold | amber
RED: purple | ruby | red | garnet | brick | brown
ROSÉ: pink | salmon | orange | copper

COLOUR DEPTH:
watery | pale | medium | deep | dark

CLARITY:
clear | slight haze | cloudy

AROMA INTENSITY:
low | moderate | aromatic | powerful

DEVELOPMENT:
youthful | some age | aged

AROMAS:

DRY/SWEET:
bone dry | dry | off dry | medium sweet | sweet | very sweet

BODY:
very light | light | medium | medium-full | full-bodied | heavy

ACIDITY:
tart | crisp | lively | smooth | flabby

TANNINS (IF PRESENT):
LEVEL: low | medium | high   TYPE: soft | round | dry | hard

FLAVOUR INTENSITY:
low | moderate | flavourful | powerful

FLAVOURS:

FINISH:
short (< 3 sec) | medium (4-5) | long (5-7) | v. long (>8 sec)

CONCLUSION/BALANCE:

rating:

FOOD: **FOOD PAIRING:**
                  MATCH: perfect | good | neutral | bad

tasting date: location:

tasting partner(s):

wine name:

producer:

region/appellation:

grape varieties:

vintage: alcohol: price:

COLOUR HUE:
WHITE: greenish | yellow | straw yellow | gold | amber
RED: purple | ruby | red | garnet | brick | brown
ROSÉ: pink | salmon | orange | copper

COLOUR DEPTH:
watery | pale | medium | deep | dark

CLARITY:
clear | slight haze | cloudy

AROMA INTENSITY:
low | moderate | aromatic | powerful

DEVELOPMENT:
youthful | some age | aged

AROMAS:

DRY/SWEET:
bone dry | dry | off dry | medium sweet | sweet | very sweet

BODY:
very light | light | medium | medium-full | full-bodied | heavy

ACIDITY:
tart | crisp | lively | smooth | flabby

TANNINS (IF PRESENT):
LEVEL: low | medium | high   TYPE: soft | round | dry | hard

FLAVOUR INTENSITY:
low | moderate | flavourful | powerful

FLAVOURS:

FINISH:
short (< 3 sec) | medium (4-5) | long (5-7) | v. long (>8 sec)

CONCLUSION/BALANCE:

rating:

FOOD: **FOOD PAIRING:**

MATCH: perfect | good | neutral | bad

tasting date: location:

tasting partner(s):

wine name:

producer:

region/appellation:

grape varieties:

vintage: alcohol: price:

COLOUR HUE:
WHITE: greenish | yellow | straw yellow | gold | amber
RED: purple | ruby | red | garnet | brick | brown
ROSÉ: pink | salmon | orange | copper

COLOUR DEPTH:
watery | pale | medium | deep | dark

CLARITY:
clear | slight haze | cloudy

AROMA INTENSITY:
low | moderate | aromatic | powerful

DEVELOPMENT:
youthful | some age | aged

AROMAS:

DRY/SWEET:
bone dry | dry | off dry | medium sweet | sweet | very sweet

BODY:
very light | light | medium | medium-full | full-bodied | heavy

ACIDITY:
tart | crisp | lively | smooth | flabby

TANNINS (IF PRESENT):
LEVEL: low | medium | high   TYPE: soft | round | dry | hard

FLAVOUR INTENSITY:
low | moderate | flavourful | powerful

FLAVOURS:

FINISH:
short (< 3 sec) | medium (4-5) | long (5-7) | v. long (>8 sec)

CONCLUSION/BALANCE:

rating:

FOOD: **FOOD PAIRING:**

MATCH: perfect | good | neutral | bad

tasting date: location:

tasting partner(s):

wine name:

producer:

region/appellation:

grape varieties:

vintage: alcohol: price:

COLOUR HUE:
WHITE: greenish | yellow | straw yellow | gold | amber
RED: purple | ruby | red | garnet | brick | brown
ROSÉ: pink | salmon | orange | copper

COLOUR DEPTH:
watery | pale | medium | deep | dark

CLARITY:
clear | slight haze | cloudy

AROMA INTENSITY:
low | moderate | aromatic | powerful

DEVELOPMENT:
youthful | some age | aged

AROMAS:

DRY/SWEET:
bone dry | dry | off dry | medium sweet | sweet | very sweet

BODY:
very light | light | medium | medium-full | full-bodied | heavy

ACIDITY:
tart | crisp | lively | smooth | flabby

TANNINS (IF PRESENT):
LEVEL: low | medium | high   TYPE: soft | round | dry | hard

FLAVOUR INTENSITY:
low | moderate | flavourful | powerful

FLAVOURS:

FINISH:
short (< 3 sec) | medium (4-5) | long (5-7) | v. long (>8 sec)

CONCLUSION/BALANCE:

rating:

FOOD:

FOOD PAIRING:
MATCH: perfect | good | neutral | bad

tasting date: location:

tasting partner(s):

wine name:

producer:

region/appellation:

grape varieties:

vintage: alcohol: price:

COLOUR HUE:

WHITE: greenish | yellow | straw yellow | gold | amber
RED: purple | ruby | red | garnet | brick | brown
ROSÉ: pink | salmon | orange | copper

COLOUR DEPTH:
watery | pale | medium | deep | dark

CLARITY:
clear | slight haze | cloudy

AROMA INTENSITY:
low | moderate | aromatic | powerful

DEVELOPMENT:
youthful | some age | aged

AROMAS:

DRY/SWEET:
bone dry | dry | off dry | medium sweet | sweet | very sweet

BODY:
very light | light | medium | medium-full | full-bodied | heavy

ACIDITY:
tart | crisp | lively | smooth | flabby

TANNINS (IF PRESENT):
LEVEL: low | medium | high   TYPE: soft | round | dry | hard

FLAVOUR INTENSITY:
low | moderate | flavourful | powerful

FLAVOURS:

FINISH:
short (< 3 sec) | medium (4-5) | long (5-7) | v. long (>8 sec)

CONCLUSION/BALANCE:

rating:

FOOD: **FOOD PAIRING:**

MATCH: perfect | good | neutral | bad

tasting date: location:

tasting partner(s):

wine name:

producer:

region/appellation:

grape varieties:

vintage: alcohol: price:

COLOUR HUE:
WHITE: greenish | yellow | straw yellow | gold | amber
RED: purple | ruby | red | garnet | brick | brown
ROSÉ: pink | salmon | orange | copper

COLOUR DEPTH:
watery | pale | medium | deep | dark

CLARITY:
clear | slight haze | cloudy

AROMA INTENSITY:
low | moderate | aromatic | powerful

DEVELOPMENT:
youthful | some age | aged

AROMAS:

DRY/SWEET:
bone dry | dry | off dry | medium sweet | sweet | very sweet

BODY:
very light | light | medium | medium-full | full-bodied | heavy

ACIDITY:
tart | crisp | lively | smooth | flabby

TANNINS (IF PRESENT):
LEVEL: low | medium | high   TYPE: soft | round | dry | hard

FLAVOUR INTENSITY:
low | moderate | flavourful | powerful

FLAVOURS:

FINISH:
short (< 3 sec) | medium (4-5) | long (5-7) | v. long (>8 sec)

CONCLUSION/BALANCE:

rating:

FOOD: **FOOD PAIRING:**
                MATCH: perfect | good | neutral | bad

tasting date: location:

tasting partner(s):

wine name:

producer:

region/appellation:

grape varieties:

vintage: alcohol: price:

COLOUR HUE:
WHITE: greenish | yellow | straw yellow | gold | amber
RED: purple | ruby | red | garnet | brick | brown
ROSÉ: pink | salmon | orange | copper

COLOUR DEPTH:
watery | pale | medium | deep | dark

CLARITY:
clear | slight haze | cloudy

AROMA INTENSITY:
low | moderate | aromatic | powerful

DEVELOPMENT:
youthful | some age | aged

AROMAS:

DRY/SWEET:
bone dry | dry | off dry | medium sweet | sweet | very sweet

BODY:
very light | light | medium | medium-full | full-bodied | heavy

ACIDITY:
tart | crisp | lively | smooth | flabby

TANNINS (IF PRESENT):
LEVEL: low | medium | high   TYPE: soft | round | dry | hard

FLAVOUR INTENSITY:
low | moderate | flavourful | powerful

FLAVOURS:

FINISH:
short (< 3 sec) | medium (4-5) | long (5-7) | v. long (>8 sec)

CONCLUSION/BALANCE:

rating:

FOOD: **FOOD PAIRING:**
                        MATCH: perfect | good | neutral | bad

tasting date: location:

tasting partner(s):

wine name:

producer:

region/appellation:

grape varieties:

vintage: alcohol: price:

COLOUR HUE:

WHITE: greenish | yellow | straw yellow | gold | amber
RED: purple | ruby | red | garnet | brick | brown
ROSÉ: pink | salmon | orange | copper

COLOUR DEPTH:
watery | pale | medium | deep | dark

CLARITY:
clear | slight haze | cloudy

AROMA INTENSITY:
low | moderate | aromatic | powerful

DEVELOPMENT:
youthful | some age | aged

AROMAS:

DRY/SWEET:
bone dry | dry | off dry | medium sweet | sweet | very sweet

BODY:
very light | light | medium | medium-full | full-bodied | heavy

ACIDITY:
tart | crisp | lively | smooth | flabby

TANNINS (IF PRESENT):
LEVEL: low | medium | high   TYPE: soft | round | dry | hard

FLAVOUR INTENSITY:
low | moderate | flavourful | powerful

FLAVOURS:

FINISH:
short (< 3 sec) | medium (4-5) | long (5-7) | v. long (>8 sec)

CONCLUSION/BALANCE:

rating:

FOOD: **FOOD PAIRING:**
                  MATCH: perfect | good | neutral | bad

tasting date: location:

tasting partner(s):

wine name:

producer:

region/appellation:

grape varieties:

vintage: alcohol: price:

COLOUR HUE:
WHITE: greenish | yellow | straw yellow | gold | amber
RED: purple | ruby | red | garnet | brick | brown
ROSÉ: pink | salmon | orange | copper

COLOUR DEPTH:
watery | pale | medium | deep | dark

CLARITY:
clear | slight haze | cloudy

AROMA INTENSITY:
low | moderate | aromatic | powerful

DEVELOPMENT:
youthful | some age | aged

AROMAS:

DRY/SWEET:
bone dry | dry | off dry | medium sweet | sweet | very sweet

BODY:
very light | light | medium | medium-full | full-bodied | heavy

ACIDITY:
tart | crisp | lively | smooth | flabby

TANNINS (IF PRESENT):
LEVEL: low | medium | high   TYPE: soft | round | dry | hard

FLAVOUR INTENSITY:
low | moderate | flavourful | powerful

FLAVOURS:

FINISH:
short (< 3 sec) | medium (4-5) | long (5-7) | v. long (>8 sec)

CONCLUSION/BALANCE:

rating:

FOOD: **FOOD PAIRING:**
                   MATCH: perfect | good | neutral | bad

tasting date: location:

tasting partner(s):

wine name:

producer:

region/appellation:

grape varieties:

vintage: alcohol: price:

COLOUR HUE:

 WHITE: greenish | yellow | straw yellow | gold | amber
RED: purple | ruby | red | garnet | brick | brown
ROSÉ: pink | salmon | orange | copper

COLOUR DEPTH:
watery | pale | medium | deep | dark

CLARITY:
clear | slight haze | cloudy

AROMA INTENSITY:
low | moderate | aromatic | powerful

DEVELOPMENT:
youthful | some age | aged

AROMAS:

DRY/SWEET:
bone dry | dry | off dry | medium sweet | sweet | very sweet

BODY:
very light | light | medium | medium-full | full-bodied | heavy

ACIDITY:
tart | crisp | lively | smooth | flabby

TANNINS (IF PRESENT):
LEVEL: low | medium | high   TYPE: soft | round | dry | hard

FLAVOUR INTENSITY:
low | moderate | flavourful | powerful

FLAVOURS: ˙

FINISH:
short (< 3 sec) | medium (4-5) | long (5-7) | v. long (>8 sec)

CONCLUSION/BALANCE:

rating:

FOOD: **FOOD PAIRING:**
              MATCH: perfect | good | neutral | bad

tasting date: location:

tasting partner(s):

wine name:

producer:

region/appellation:

grape varieties:

vintage: alcohol: price:

COLOUR HUE:
WHITE: greenish | yellow | straw yellow | gold | amber
RED: purple | ruby | red | garnet | brick | brown
ROSÉ: pink | salmon | orange | copper

COLOUR DEPTH:
watery | pale | medium | deep | dark

CLARITY:
clear | slight haze | cloudy

AROMA INTENSITY:
low | moderate | aromatic | powerful

DEVELOPMENT:
youthful | some age | aged

AROMAS:

DRY/SWEET:
bone dry | dry | off dry | medium sweet | sweet | very sweet

BODY:
very light | light | medium | medium-full | full-bodied | heavy

ACIDITY:
tart | crisp | lively | smooth | flabby

TANNINS (IF PRESENT):
LEVEL: low | medium | high   TYPE: soft | round | dry | hard

FLAVOUR INTENSITY:
low | moderate | flavourful | powerful

FLAVOURS:

FINISH:
short (< 3 sec) | medium (4-5) | long (5-7) | v. long (>8 sec)

CONCLUSION/BALANCE:

rating:

FOOD: **FOOD PAIRING:**
MATCH: perfect | good | neutral | bad

tasting date: location:

tasting partner(s):

wine name:

producer:

region/appellation:

grape varieties:

vintage: alcohol: price:

COLOUR HUE:
WHITE: greenish | yellow | straw yellow | gold | amber
RED: purple | ruby | red | garnet | brick | brown
ROSÉ: pink | salmon | orange | copper

COLOUR DEPTH:
watery | pale | medium | deep | dark

CLARITY:
clear | slight haze | cloudy

AROMA INTENSITY:
low | moderate | aromatic | powerful

DEVELOPMENT:
youthful | some age | aged

AROMAS:

DRY/SWEET:
bone dry | dry | off dry | medium sweet | sweet | very sweet

BODY:
very light | light | medium | medium-full | full-bodied | heavy

ACIDITY:
tart | crisp | lively | smooth | flabby

TANNINS (IF PRESENT):
LEVEL: low | medium | high   TYPE: soft | round | dry | hard

FLAVOUR INTENSITY:
low | moderate | flavourful | powerful

FLAVOURS:

FINISH:
short (< 3 sec) | medium (4-5) | long (5-7) | v. long (>8 sec)

CONCLUSION/BALANCE:

rating:

FOOD: **FOOD PAIRING:**
                MATCH: perfect | good | neutral | bad

tasting date: location:

tasting partner(s):

wine name:

producer:

region/appellation:

grape varieties:

vintage: alcohol: price:

COLOUR HUE:

WHITE: greenish | yellow | straw yellow | gold | amber
RED: purple | ruby | red | garnet | brick | brown
ROSÉ: pink | salmon | orange | copper

COLOUR DEPTH:
watery | pale | medium | deep | dark

CLARITY:
clear | slight haze | cloudy

AROMA INTENSITY:
low | moderate | aromatic | powerful

DEVELOPMENT:
youthful | some age | aged

AROMAS:

DRY/SWEET:
bone dry | dry | off dry | medium sweet | sweet | very sweet

BODY:
very light | light | medium | medium-full | full-bodied | heavy

ACIDITY:
tart | crisp | lively | smooth | flabby

TANNINS (IF PRESENT):
LEVEL: low | medium | high   TYPE: soft | round | dry | hard

FLAVOUR INTENSITY:
low | moderate | flavourful | powerful

FLAVOURS:

FINISH:
short (< 3 sec) | medium (4-5) | long (5-7) | v. long (>8 sec)

CONCLUSION/BALANCE:

rating:

FOOD: ### FOOD PAIRING:
                MATCH: perfect | good | neutral | bad

tasting date: location:

tasting partner(s):

wine name:

producer:

region/appellation:

grape varieties:

vintage: alcohol: price:

COLOUR HUE:
WHITE: greenish | yellow | straw yellow | gold | amber
RED: purple | ruby | red | garnet | brick | brown
ROSÉ: pink | salmon | orange | copper

COLOUR DEPTH:
watery | pale | medium | deep | dark

CLARITY:
clear | slight haze | cloudy

AROMA INTENSITY:
low | moderate | aromatic | powerful

DEVELOPMENT:
youthful | some age | aged

AROMAS:

DRY/SWEET:
bone dry | dry | off dry | medium sweet | sweet | very sweet

BODY:
very light | light | medium | medium-full | full-bodied | heavy

ACIDITY:
tart | crisp | lively | smooth | flabby

TANNINS (IF PRESENT):
LEVEL: low | medium | high   TYPE: soft | round | dry | hard

FLAVOUR INTENSITY:
low | moderate | flavourful | powerful

FLAVOURS:

FINISH:
short (< 3 sec) | medium (4-5) | long (5-7) | v. long (>8 sec)

CONCLUSION/BALANCE:

rating:

FOOD: **FOOD PAIRING:**
                    MATCH: perfect | good | neutral | bad

tasting date: location:

tasting partner(s):

wine name:

producer:

region/appellation:

grape varieties:

vintage: alcohol: price:

COLOUR HUE:

WHITE: greenish | yellow | straw yellow | gold | amber
RED: purple | ruby | red | garnet | brick | brown
ROSÉ: pink | salmon | orange | copper

COLOUR DEPTH:
watery | pale | medium | deep | dark

CLARITY:
clear | slight haze | cloudy

AROMA INTENSITY:
low | moderate | aromatic | powerful

DEVELOPMENT:
youthful | some age | aged

AROMAS:

DRY/SWEET:
bone dry | dry | off dry | medium sweet | sweet | very sweet

BODY:
very light | light | medium | medium-full | full-bodied | heavy

ACIDITY:
tart | crisp | lively | smooth | flabby

TANNINS (IF PRESENT):
LEVEL: low | medium | high   TYPE: soft | round | dry | hard

FLAVOUR INTENSITY:
low | moderate | flavourful | powerful

FLAVOURS:

FINISH:
short (< 3 sec) | medium (4-5) | long (5-7) | v. long (>8 sec)

CONCLUSION/BALANCE:

rating:

FOOD: **FOOD PAIRING:**

MATCH: perfect | good | neutral | bad

tasting date: location:

tasting partner(s):

wine name:

producer:

region/appellation:

grape varieties:

vintage: alcohol: price:

COLOUR HUE:
WHITE: greenish | yellow | straw yellow | gold | amber
RED: purple | ruby | red | garnet | brick | brown
ROSÉ: pink | salmon | orange | copper

COLOUR DEPTH:
watery | pale | medium | deep | dark

CLARITY:
clear | slight haze | cloudy

AROMA INTENSITY:
low | moderate | aromatic | powerful

DEVELOPMENT:
youthful | some age | aged

AROMAS:

DRY/SWEET:
bone dry | dry | off dry | medium sweet | sweet | very sweet

BODY:
very light | light | medium | medium-full | full-bodied | heavy

ACIDITY:
tart | crisp | lively | smooth | flabby

TANNINS (IF PRESENT):
LEVEL: low | medium | high   TYPE: soft | round | dry | hard

FLAVOUR INTENSITY:
low | moderate | flavourful | powerful

FLAVOURS:

FINISH:
short (< 3 sec) | medium (4-5) | long (5-7) | v. long (>8 sec)

CONCLUSION/BALANCE:

rating:

FOOD: **FOOD PAIRING:**
                 MATCH: perfect | good | neutral | bad

tasting date: location:

tasting partner(s):

wine name:

producer:

region/appellation:

grape varieties:

vintage: alcohol: price:

COLOUR HUE:

WHITE: greenish | yellow | straw yellow | gold | amber
RED: purple | ruby | red | garnet | brick | brown
ROSÉ: pink | salmon | orange | copper

COLOUR DEPTH:
watery | pale | medium | deep | dark

CLARITY:
clear | slight haze | cloudy

AROMA INTENSITY:
low | moderate | aromatic | powerful

DEVELOPMENT:
youthful | some age | aged

AROMAS:

DRY/SWEET:

bone dry | dry | off dry | medium sweet | sweet | very sweet

BODY:
very light | light | medium | medium-full | full-bodied | heavy

ACIDITY:
tart | crisp | lively | smooth | flabby

TANNINS (IF PRESENT):
LEVEL: low | medium | high   TYPE: soft | round | dry | hard

FLAVOUR INTENSITY:
low | moderate | flavourful | powerful

FLAVOURS:

FINISH:
short (< 3 sec) | medium (4-5) | long (5-7) | v. long (>8 sec)

CONCLUSION/BALANCE:

rating:

FOOD: **FOOD PAIRING:**

MATCH: perfect | good | neutral | bad

tasting date: location:

tasting partner(s):

wine name:

producer:

region/appellation:

grape varieties:

vintage: alcohol: price:

COLOUR HUE:

WHITE: greenish | yellow | straw yellow | gold | amber
RED: purple | ruby | red | garnet | brick | brown
ROSÉ: pink | salmon | orange | copper

COLOUR DEPTH:
watery | pale | medium | deep | dark

CLARITY:
clear | slight haze | cloudy

AROMA INTENSITY:
low | moderate | aromatic | powerful

DEVELOPMENT:
youthful | some age | aged

AROMAS:

DRY/SWEET:
bone dry | dry | off dry | medium sweet | sweet | very sweet

BODY:
very light | light | medium | medium-full | full-bodied | heavy

ACIDITY:
tart | crisp | lively | smooth | flabby

TANNINS (IF PRESENT):
LEVEL: low | medium | high   TYPE: soft | round | dry | hard

FLAVOUR INTENSITY:
low | moderate | flavourful | powerful

FLAVOURS:

FINISH:
short (< 3 sec) | medium (4-5) | long (5-7) | v. long (>8 sec)

CONCLUSION/BALANCE:

rating:

FOOD: **FOOD PAIRING:**

MATCH: perfect | good | neutral | bad

tasting date: location:

tasting partner(s):

wine name:

producer:

region/appellation:

grape varieties:

vintage: alcohol: price:

COLOUR HUE:
WHITE: greenish | yellow | straw yellow | gold | amber
RED: purple | ruby | red | garnet | brick | brown
ROSÉ: pink | salmon | orange | copper

COLOUR DEPTH:
watery | pale | medium | deep | dark

CLARITY:
clear | slight haze | cloudy

AROMA INTENSITY:
low | moderate | aromatic | powerful

DEVELOPMENT:
youthful | some age | aged

AROMAS:

DRY/SWEET:
bone dry | dry | off dry | medium sweet | sweet | very sweet

BODY:
very light | light | medium | medium-full | full-bodied | heavy

ACIDITY:
tart | crisp | lively | smooth | flabby

TANNINS (IF PRESENT):
LEVEL: low | medium | high   TYPE: soft | round | dry | hard

FLAVOUR INTENSITY:
low | moderate | flavourful | powerful

FLAVOURS:

FINISH:
short (< 3 sec) | medium (4-5) | long (5-7) | v. long (>8 sec)

CONCLUSION/BALANCE:

rating:

FOOD: **FOOD PAIRING:**
                    MATCH: perfect | good | neutral | bad

tasting date: location:

tasting partner(s):

wine name:

producer:

region/appellation:

grape varieties:

vintage: alcohol: price:

COLOUR HUE:
WHITE: greenish | yellow | straw yellow | gold | amber
RED: purple | ruby | red | garnet | brick | brown
ROSÉ: pink | salmon | orange | copper

COLOUR DEPTH:
watery | pale | medium | deep | dark

CLARITY:
clear | slight haze | cloudy

AROMA INTENSITY:
low | moderate | aromatic | powerful

DEVELOPMENT:
youthful | some age | aged

AROMAS:

DRY/SWEET:
bone dry | dry | off dry | medium sweet | sweet | very sweet

BODY:
very light | light | medium | medium-full | full-bodied | heavy

ACIDITY:
tart | crisp | lively | smooth | flabby

TANNINS (IF PRESENT):
LEVEL: low | medium | high   TYPE: soft | round | dry | hard

FLAVOUR INTENSITY:
low | moderate | flavourful | powerful

FLAVOURS:

FINISH:
short (< 3 sec) | medium (4-5) | long (5-7) | v. long (>8 sec)

CONCLUSION/BALANCE:

rating:

FOOD: **FOOD PAIRING:**
                    MATCH: perfect | good | neutral | bad

tasting date: location:

tasting partner(s):

wine name:

producer:

region/appellation:

grape varieties:

vintage: alcohol: price:

COLOUR HUE:
WHITE: greenish | yellow | straw yellow | gold | amber
RED: purple | ruby | red | garnet | brick | brown
ROSÉ: pink | salmon | orange | copper

COLOUR DEPTH:
watery | pale | medium | deep | dark

CLARITY:
clear | slight haze | cloudy

AROMA INTENSITY:
low | moderate | aromatic | powerful

DEVELOPMENT:
youthful | some age | aged

AROMAS:

DRY/SWEET:
bone dry | dry | off dry | medium sweet | sweet | very sweet

BODY:
very light | light | medium | medium-full | full-bodied | heavy

ACIDITY:
tart | crisp | lively | smooth | flabby

TANNINS (IF PRESENT):
LEVEL: low | medium | high   TYPE: soft | round | dry | hard

FLAVOUR INTENSITY:
low | moderate | flavourful | powerful

FLAVOURS:

FINISH:
short (< 3 sec) | medium (4-5) | long (5-7) | v. long (>8 sec)

CONCLUSION/BALANCE:

rating:

FOOD: **FOOD PAIRING:**

MATCH: perfect | good | neutral | bad

tasting date: location:

tasting partner(s):

wine name:

producer:

region/appellation:

grape varieties:

vintage: alcohol: price:

COLOUR HUE:
WHITE: greenish | yellow | straw yellow | gold | amber
RED: purple | ruby | red | garnet | brick | brown
ROSÉ: pink | salmon | orange | copper

COLOUR DEPTH:
watery | pale | medium | deep | dark

CLARITY:
clear | slight haze | cloudy

AROMA INTENSITY:
low | moderate | aromatic | powerful

DEVELOPMENT:
youthful | some age | aged

AROMAS:

DRY/SWEET:
bone dry | dry | off dry | medium sweet | sweet | very sweet

BODY:
very light | light | medium | medium-full | full-bodied | heavy

ACIDITY:
tart | crisp | lively | smooth | flabby

TANNINS (IF PRESENT):
LEVEL: low | medium | high   TYPE: soft | round | dry | hard

FLAVOUR INTENSITY:
low | moderate | flavourful | powerful

FLAVOURS:

FINISH:
short (< 3 sec) | medium (4-5) | long (5-7) | v. long (>8 sec)

CONCLUSION/BALANCE:

rating:

FOOD: **FOOD PAIRING:**

                     MATCH: perfect | good | neutral | bad

tasting date: location:

tasting partner(s):

wine name:

producer:

region/appellation:

grape varieties:

vintage: alcohol: price:

COLOUR HUE:
WHITE: greenish | yellow | straw yellow | gold | amber
RED: purple | ruby | red | garnet | brick | brown
ROSÉ: pink | salmon | orange | copper

COLOUR DEPTH:
watery | pale | medium | deep | dark

CLARITY:
clear | slight haze | cloudy

AROMA INTENSITY:
low | moderate | aromatic | powerful

DEVELOPMENT:
youthful | some age | aged

AROMAS:

DRY/SWEET:
bone dry | dry | off dry | medium sweet | sweet | very sweet

BODY:
very light | light | medium | medium-full | full-bodied | heavy

ACIDITY:
tart | crisp | lively | smooth | flabby

TANNINS (IF PRESENT):
LEVEL: low | medium | high   TYPE: soft | round | dry | hard

FLAVOUR INTENSITY:
low | moderate | flavourful | powerful

FLAVOURS:

FINISH:
short (< 3 sec) | medium (4-5) | long (5-7) | v. long (>8 sec)

CONCLUSION/BALANCE:

rating:

FOOD: **FOOD PAIRING:**
                MATCH: perfect | good | neutral | bad

tasting date: location:

tasting partner(s):

wine name:

producer:

region/appellation:

grape varieties:

vintage: alcohol: price:

COLOUR HUE:
WHITE: greenish | yellow | straw yellow | gold | amber
RED: purple | ruby | red | garnet | brick | brown
ROSÉ: pink | salmon | orange | copper

COLOUR DEPTH:
watery | pale | medium | deep | dark

CLARITY:
clear | slight haze | cloudy

AROMA INTENSITY:
low | moderate | aromatic | powerful

DEVELOPMENT:
youthful | some age | aged

AROMAS:

DRY/SWEET:
bone dry | dry | off dry | medium sweet | sweet | very sweet

BODY:
very light | light | medium | medium-full | full-bodied | heavy

ACIDITY:
tart | crisp | lively | smooth | flabby

TANNINS (IF PRESENT):
LEVEL: low | medium | high   TYPE: soft | round | dry | hard

FLAVOUR INTENSITY:
low | moderate | flavourful | powerful

FLAVOURS:

FINISH:
short (< 3 sec) | medium (4-5) | long (5-7) | v. long (>8 sec)

CONCLUSION/BALANCE:

rating:

FOOD: **FOOD PAIRING:**
               MATCH: perfect | good | neutral | bad

tasting date: location:

tasting partner(s):

wine name:

producer:

region/appellation:

grape varieties:

vintage: alcohol: price:

COLOUR HUE:
WHITE: greenish | yellow | straw yellow | gold | amber
RED: purple | ruby | red | garnet | brick | brown
ROSÉ: pink | salmon | orange | copper

COLOUR DEPTH:
watery | pale | medium | deep | dark

CLARITY:
clear | slight haze | cloudy

AROMA INTENSITY:
low | moderate | aromatic | powerful

DEVELOPMENT:
youthful | some age | aged

AROMAS:

DRY/SWEET:
bone dry | dry | off dry | medium sweet | sweet | very sweet

BODY:
very light | light | medium | medium-full | full-bodied | heavy

ACIDITY:
tart | crisp | lively | smooth | flabby

TANNINS (IF PRESENT):
LEVEL: low | medium | high   TYPE: soft | round | dry | hard

FLAVOUR INTENSITY:
low | moderate | flavourful | powerful

FLAVOURS:

FINISH:
short (< 3 sec) | medium (4-5) | long (5-7) | v. long (>8 sec)

CONCLUSION/BALANCE:

rating:

FOOD: **FOOD PAIRING:**
                MATCH: perfect | good | neutral | bad

tasting date: location:

tasting partner(s):

wine name:

producer:

region/appellation:

grape varieties:

vintage: alcohol: price:

COLOUR HUE:
WHITE: greenish | yellow | straw yellow | gold | amber
RED: purple | ruby | red | garnet | brick | brown
ROSÉ: pink | salmon | orange | copper

COLOUR DEPTH:
watery | pale | medium | deep | dark

CLARITY:
clear | slight haze | cloudy

AROMA INTENSITY:
low | moderate | aromatic | powerful

DEVELOPMENT:
youthful | some age | aged

AROMAS:

DRY/SWEET:
bone dry | dry | off dry | medium sweet | sweet | very sweet

BODY:
very light | light | medium | medium-full | full-bodied | heavy

ACIDITY:
tart | crisp | lively | smooth | flabby

TANNINS (IF PRESENT):
LEVEL: low | medium | high   TYPE: soft | round | dry | hard

FLAVOUR INTENSITY:
low | moderate | flavourful | powerful

FLAVOURS:

FINISH:
short (< 3 sec) | medium (4-5) | long (5-7) | v. long (>8 sec)

CONCLUSION/BALANCE:

rating:

FOOD: **FOOD PAIRING:**
                    MATCH: perfect | good | neutral | bad

tasting date: location:

tasting partner(s):

wine name:

producer:

region/appellation:

grape varieties:

vintage: alcohol: price:

COLOUR HUE:

WHITE: greenish | yellow | straw yellow | gold | amber
RED: purple | ruby | red | garnet | brick | brown
ROSÉ: pink | salmon | orange | copper

COLOUR DEPTH:
watery | pale | medium | deep | dark

CLARITY:
clear | slight haze | cloudy

AROMA INTENSITY:
low | moderate | aromatic | powerful

DEVELOPMENT:
youthful | some age | aged

AROMAS:

DRY/SWEET:
bone dry | dry | off dry | medium sweet | sweet | very sweet

BODY:
very light | light | medium | medium-full | full-bodied | heavy

ACIDITY:
tart | crisp | lively | smooth | flabby

TANNINS (IF PRESENT):
LEVEL: low | medium | high   TYPE: soft | round | dry | hard

FLAVOUR INTENSITY:
low | moderate | flavourful | powerful

FLAVOURS:

FINISH:
short (< 3 sec) | medium (4-5) | long (5-7) | v. long (>8 sec)

CONCLUSION/BALANCE:

rating:

FOOD: **FOOD PAIRING:**
                  MATCH: perfect | good | neutral | bad

tasting date: location:

tasting partner(s):

wine name:

producer:

region/appellation:

grape varieties:

vintage: alcohol: price:

COLOUR HUE:
WHITE: greenish | yellow | straw yellow | gold | amber
RED: purple | ruby | red | garnet | brick | brown
ROSÉ: pink | salmon | orange | copper

COLOUR DEPTH:
watery | pale | medium | deep | dark

CLARITY:
clear | slight haze | cloudy

AROMA INTENSITY:
low | moderate | aromatic | powerful

DEVELOPMENT:
youthful | some age | aged

AROMAS:

DRY/SWEET:
bone dry | dry | off dry | medium sweet | sweet | very sweet

BODY:
very light | light | medium | medium-full | full-bodied | heavy

ACIDITY:
tart | crisp | lively | smooth | flabby

TANNINS (IF PRESENT):
LEVEL: low | medium | high   TYPE: soft | round | dry | hard

FLAVOUR INTENSITY:
low | moderate | flavourful | powerful

FLAVOURS:

FINISH:
short (< 3 sec) | medium (4-5) | long (5-7) | v. long (>8 sec)

CONCLUSION/BALANCE:

rating:

FOOD: **FOOD PAIRING:**
                   MATCH: perfect | good | neutral | bad

tasting date: location:

tasting partner(s):

wine name:

producer:

region/appellation:

grape varieties:

vintage: alcohol: price:

COLOUR HUE:
WHITE: greenish | yellow | straw yellow | gold | amber
RED: purple | ruby | red | garnet | brick | brown
ROSÉ: pink | salmon | orange | copper

COLOUR DEPTH:
watery | pale | medium | deep | dark

CLARITY:
clear | slight haze | cloudy

AROMA INTENSITY:
low | moderate | aromatic | powerful

DEVELOPMENT:
youthful | some age | aged

AROMAS:

DRY/SWEET:
bone dry | dry | off dry | medium sweet | sweet | very sweet

BODY:
very light | light | medium | medium-full | full-bodied | heavy

ACIDITY:
tart | crisp | lively | smooth | flabby

TANNINS (IF PRESENT):
LEVEL: low | medium | high   TYPE: soft | round | dry | hard

FLAVOUR INTENSITY:
low | moderate | flavourful | powerful

FLAVOURS:

FINISH:
short (< 3 sec) | medium (4-5) | long (5-7) | v. long (>8 sec)

CONCLUSION/BALANCE:

rating:

FOOD: **FOOD PAIRING:**
                    MATCH: perfect | good | neutral | bad

tasting date: location:

tasting partner(s):

wine name:

producer:

region/appellation:

grape varieties:

vintage: alcohol: price:

COLOUR HUE:

WHITE: greenish | yellow | straw yellow | gold | amber
RED: purple | ruby | red | garnet | brick | brown
ROSÉ: pink | salmon | orange | copper

COLOUR DEPTH:

watery | pale | medium | deep | dark

CLARITY:

clear | slight haze | cloudy

AROMA INTENSITY:

low | moderate | aromatic | powerful

DEVELOPMENT:

youthful | some age | aged

AROMAS:

DRY/SWEET:

bone dry | dry | off dry | medium sweet | sweet | very sweet

BODY:

very light | light | medium | medium-full | full-bodied | heavy

ACIDITY:

tart | crisp | lively | smooth | flabby

TANNINS (IF PRESENT):

LEVEL: low | medium | high   TYPE: soft | round | dry | hard

FLAVOUR INTENSITY:

low | moderate | flavourful | powerful

FLAVOURS:

FINISH:

short (< 3 sec) | medium (4-5) | long (5-7) | v. long (>8 sec)

CONCLUSION/BALANCE:

rating:

FOOD: **FOOD PAIRING:**

MATCH: perfect | good | neutral | bad

tasting date: location:

tasting partner(s):

wine name:

producer:

region/appellation:

grape varieties:

vintage: alcohol: price:

COLOUR HUE:

WHITE: greenish | yellow | straw yellow | gold | amber
RED: purple | ruby | red | garnet | brick | brown
ROSÉ: pink | salmon | orange | copper

COLOUR DEPTH:

watery | pale | medium | deep | dark

CLARITY:

clear | slight haze | cloudy

AROMA INTENSITY:

low | moderate | aromatic | powerful

DEVELOPMENT:

youthful | some age | aged

AROMAS:

DRY/SWEET:

bone dry | dry | off dry | medium sweet | sweet | very sweet

BODY:

very light | light | medium | medium-full | full-bodied | heavy

ACIDITY:

tart | crisp | lively | smooth | flabby

TANNINS (IF PRESENT):

LEVEL: low | medium | high   TYPE: soft | round | dry | hard

FLAVOUR INTENSITY:

low | moderate | flavourful | powerful

FLAVOURS:

FINISH:

short (< 3 sec) | medium (4-5) | long (5-7) | v. long (>8 sec)

CONCLUSION/BALANCE:

rating:

FOOD: **FOOD PAIRING:**

MATCH: perfect | good | neutral | bad

tasting date: location:

tasting partner(s):

wine name:

producer:

region/appellation:

grape varieties:

vintage: alcohol: price:

COLOUR HUE:

WHITE: greenish | yellow | straw yellow | gold | amber
RED: purple | ruby | red | garnet | brick | brown
ROSÉ: pink | salmon | orange | copper

COLOUR DEPTH:
watery | pale | medium | deep | dark

CLARITY:
clear | slight haze | cloudy

AROMA INTENSITY:
low | moderate | aromatic | powerful

DEVELOPMENT:
youthful | some age | aged

AROMAS:

DRY/SWEET:
bone dry | dry | off dry | medium sweet | sweet | very sweet

BODY:
very light | light | medium | medium-full | full-bodied | heavy

ACIDITY:
tart | crisp | lively | smooth | flabby

TANNINS (IF PRESENT):
LEVEL: low | medium | high   TYPE: soft | round | dry | hard

FLAVOUR INTENSITY:
low | moderate | flavourful | powerful

FLAVOURS:

FINISH:
short (< 3 sec) | medium (4-5) | long (5-7) | v. long (>8 sec)

CONCLUSION/BALANCE:

rating:

FOOD: **FOOD PAIRING:**
                 MATCH: perfect | good | neutral | bad

tasting date: location:

tasting partner(s):

wine name:

producer:

region/appellation:

grape varieties:

vintage: alcohol: price:

COLOUR HUE:
WHITE: greenish | yellow | straw yellow | gold | amber
RED: purple | ruby | red | garnet | brick | brown
ROSÉ: pink | salmon | orange | copper

COLOUR DEPTH:
watery | pale | medium | deep | dark

CLARITY:
clear | slight haze | cloudy

AROMA INTENSITY:
low | moderate | aromatic | powerful

DEVELOPMENT:
youthful | some age | aged

AROMAS:

DRY/SWEET:
bone dry | dry | off dry | medium sweet | sweet | very sweet

BODY:
very light | light | medium | medium-full | full-bodied | heavy

ACIDITY:
tart | crisp | lively | smooth | flabby

TANNINS (IF PRESENT):
LEVEL: low | medium | high   TYPE: soft | round | dry | hard

FLAVOUR INTENSITY:
low | moderate | flavourful | powerful

FLAVOURS:

FINISH:
short (< 3 sec) | medium (4-5) | long (5-7) | v. long (>8 sec)

CONCLUSION/BALANCE:

rating:

FOOD: **FOOD PAIRING:**
MATCH: perfect | good | neutral | bad

tasting date: location:

tasting partner(s):

wine name:

producer:

region/appellation:

grape varieties:

vintage: alcohol: price:

COLOUR HUE:
WHITE: greenish | yellow | straw yellow | gold | amber
RED: purple | ruby | red | garnet | brick | brown
ROSÉ: pink | salmon | orange | copper

COLOUR DEPTH:
watery | pale | medium | deep | dark

CLARITY:
clear | slight haze | cloudy

AROMA INTENSITY:
low | moderate | aromatic | powerful

DEVELOPMENT:
youthful | some age | aged

AROMAS:

DRY/SWEET:
bone dry | dry | off dry | medium sweet | sweet | very sweet

BODY:
very light | light | medium | medium-full | full-bodied | heavy

ACIDITY:
tart | crisp | lively | smooth | flabby

TANNINS (IF PRESENT):
LEVEL: low | medium | high   TYPE: soft | round | dry | hard

FLAVOUR INTENSITY:
low | moderate | flavourful | powerful

FLAVOURS: '

FINISH:
short (< 3 sec) | medium (4-5) | long (5-7) | v. long (>8 sec)

CONCLUSION/BALANCE:

rating:

FOOD:

FOOD PAIRING:
MATCH: perfect | good | neutral | bad

tasting date: location:

tasting partner(s):

wine name:

producer:

region/appellation:

grape varieties:

vintage: alcohol: price:

COLOUR HUE:
WHITE: greenish | yellow | straw yellow | gold | amber
RED: purple | ruby | red | garnet | brick | brown
ROSÉ: pink | salmon | orange | copper

COLOUR DEPTH:
watery | pale | medium | deep | dark

CLARITY:
clear | slight haze | cloudy

AROMA INTENSITY:
low | moderate | aromatic | powerful

DEVELOPMENT:
youthful | some age | aged

AROMAS:

DRY/SWEET:
bone dry | dry | off dry | medium sweet | sweet | very sweet

BODY:
very light | light | medium | medium-full | full-bodied | heavy

ACIDITY:
tart | crisp | lively | smooth | flabby

TANNINS (IF PRESENT):
LEVEL: low | medium | high   TYPE: soft | round | dry | hard

FLAVOUR INTENSITY:
low | moderate | flavourful | powerful

FLAVOURS:

FINISH:
short (< 3 sec) | medium (4-5) | long (5-7) | v. long (>8 sec)

CONCLUSION/BALANCE:

rating:

FOOD: **FOOD PAIRING:**

MATCH: perfect | good | neutral | bad

tasting date: location:

tasting partner(s):

wine name:

producer:

region/appellation:

grape varieties:

vintage: alcohol: price:

COLOUR HUE:

WHITE: greenish | yellow | straw yellow | gold | amber
RED: purple | ruby | red | garnet | brick | brown
ROSÉ: pink | salmon | orange | copper

COLOUR DEPTH:
watery | pale | medium | deep | dark

CLARITY:
clear | slight haze | cloudy

AROMA INTENSITY:
low | moderate | aromatic | powerful

DEVELOPMENT:
youthful | some age | aged

AROMAS:

DRY/SWEET:
bone dry | dry | off dry | medium sweet | sweet | very sweet

BODY:
very light | light | medium | medium-full | full-bodied | heavy

ACIDITY:
tart | crisp | lively | smooth | flabby

TANNINS (IF PRESENT):
LEVEL: low | medium | high   TYPE: soft | round | dry | hard

FLAVOUR INTENSITY:
low | moderate | flavourful | powerful

FLAVOURS:

FINISH:
short (< 3 sec) | medium (4-5) | long (5-7) | v. long (>8 sec)

CONCLUSION/BALANCE:

rating:

FOOD: **FOOD PAIRING:**

MATCH: perfect | good | neutral | bad

tasting date: location:

tasting partner(s):

wine name:

producer:

region/appellation:

grape varieties:

vintage: alcohol: price:

COLOUR HUE:
WHITE: greenish | yellow | straw yellow | gold | amber
RED: purple | ruby | red | garnet | brick | brown
ROSÉ: pink | salmon | orange | copper

COLOUR DEPTH:
watery | pale | medium | deep | dark

CLARITY:
clear | slight haze | cloudy

AROMA INTENSITY:
low | moderate | aromatic | powerful

DEVELOPMENT:
youthful | some age | aged

AROMAS:

DRY/SWEET:
bone dry | dry | off dry | medium sweet | sweet | very sweet

BODY:
very light | light | medium | medium-full | full-bodied | heavy

ACIDITY:
tart | crisp | lively | smooth | flabby

TANNINS (IF PRESENT):
LEVEL: low | medium | high   TYPE: soft | round | dry | hard

FLAVOUR INTENSITY:
low | moderate | flavourful | powerful

FLAVOURS:

FINISH:
short (< 3 sec) | medium (4-5) | long (5-7) | v. long (>8 sec)

CONCLUSION/BALANCE:

rating:

FOOD: **FOOD PAIRING:**

MATCH: perfect | good | neutral | bad

tasting date: location:

tasting partner(s):

wine name:

producer:

region/appellation:

grape varieties:

vintage: alcohol: price:

COLOUR HUE:

WHITE: greenish | yellow | straw yellow | gold | amber
RED: purple | ruby | red | garnet | brick | brown
ROSÉ: pink | salmon | orange | copper

COLOUR DEPTH:
watery | pale | medium | deep | dark

CLARITY:
clear | slight haze | cloudy

AROMA INTENSITY:
low | moderate | aromatic | powerful

DEVELOPMENT:
youthful | some age | aged

AROMAS:

DRY/SWEET:
bone dry | dry | off dry | medium sweet | sweet | very sweet

BODY:
very light | light | medium | medium-full | full-bodied | heavy

ACIDITY:
tart | crisp | lively | smooth | flabby

TANNINS (IF PRESENT):
LEVEL: low | medium | high   TYPE: soft | round | dry | hard

FLAVOUR INTENSITY:
low | moderate | flavourful | powerful

FLAVOURS:

FINISH:
short (< 3 sec) | medium (4-5) | long (5-7) | v. long (>8 sec)

CONCLUSION/BALANCE:

rating:

FOOD: **FOOD PAIRING:**

MATCH: perfect | good | neutral | bad

tasting date: location:

tasting partner(s):

wine name:

producer:

region/appellation:

grape varieties:

vintage: alcohol: price:

COLOUR HUE:

WHITE: greenish | yellow | straw yellow | gold | amber
RED: purple | ruby | red | garnet | brick | brown
ROSÉ: pink | salmon | orange | copper

COLOUR DEPTH:
watery | pale | medium | deep | dark

CLARITY:
clear | slight haze | cloudy

AROMA INTENSITY:
low | moderate | aromatic | powerful

DEVELOPMENT:
youthful | some age | aged

AROMAS:

DRY/SWEET:
bone dry | dry | off dry | medium sweet | sweet | very sweet

BODY:
very light | light | medium | medium-full | full-bodied | heavy

ACIDITY:
tart | crisp | lively | smooth | flabby

TANNINS (IF PRESENT):
LEVEL: low | medium | high   TYPE: soft | round | dry | hard

FLAVOUR INTENSITY:
low | moderate | flavourful | powerful

FLAVOURS:

FINISH:
short (< 3 sec) | medium (4-5) | long (5-7) | v. long (>8 sec)

CONCLUSION/BALANCE:

rating:

FOOD: **FOOD PAIRING:**

MATCH: perfect | good | neutral | bad

tasting date: location:

tasting partner(s):

wine name:

producer:

region/appellation:

grape varieties:

vintage: alcohol: price:

COLOUR HUE:
WHITE: greenish | yellow | straw yellow | gold | amber
RED: purple | ruby | red | garnet | brick | brown
ROSÉ: pink | salmon | orange | copper

COLOUR DEPTH:
watery | pale | medium | deep | dark

CLARITY:
clear | slight haze | cloudy

AROMA INTENSITY:
low | moderate | aromatic | powerful

DEVELOPMENT:
youthful | some age | aged

AROMAS:

DRY/SWEET:
bone dry | dry | off dry | medium sweet | sweet | very sweet

BODY:
very light | light | medium | medium-full | full-bodied | heavy

ACIDITY:
tart | crisp | lively | smooth | flabby

TANNINS (IF PRESENT):
LEVEL: low | medium | high   TYPE: soft | round | dry | hard

FLAVOUR INTENSITY:
low | moderate | flavourful | powerful

FLAVOURS:

FINISH:
short (< 3 sec) | medium (4-5) | long (5-7) | v. long (>8 sec)

CONCLUSION/BALANCE:

rating:

FOOD: **FOOD PAIRING:**
                MATCH: perfect | good | neutral | bad

tasting date: location:

tasting partner(s):

wine name:

producer:

region/appellation:

grape varieties:

vintage: alcohol: price:

COLOUR HUE:

WHITE: greenish | yellow | straw yellow | gold | amber
RED: purple | ruby | red | garnet | brick | brown
ROSÉ: pink | salmon | orange | copper

COLOUR DEPTH:
watery | pale | medium | deep | dark

CLARITY:
clear | slight haze | cloudy

AROMA INTENSITY:
low | moderate | aromatic | powerful

DEVELOPMENT:
youthful | some age | aged

AROMAS:

DRY/SWEET:
bone dry | dry | off dry | medium sweet | sweet | very sweet

BODY:
very light | light | medium | medium-full | full-bodied | heavy

ACIDITY:
tart | crisp | lively | smooth | flabby

TANNINS (IF PRESENT):
LEVEL: low | medium | high   TYPE: soft | round | dry | hard

FLAVOUR INTENSITY:
low | moderate | flavourful | powerful

FLAVOURS:

FINISH:
short (< 3 sec) | medium (4-5) | long (5-7) | v. long (>8 sec)

CONCLUSION/BALANCE:

rating:

FOOD: **FOOD PAIRING:**

MATCH: perfect | good | neutral | bad

tasting date: location:

tasting partner(s):

wine name:

producer:

region/appellation:

grape varieties:

vintage: alcohol: price:

COLOUR HUE:

WHITE: greenish | yellow | straw yellow | gold | amber
RED: purple | ruby | red | garnet | brick | brown
ROSÉ: pink | salmon | orange | copper

COLOUR DEPTH:
watery | pale | medium | deep | dark

CLARITY:
clear | slight haze | cloudy

AROMA INTENSITY:
low | moderate | aromatic | powerful

DEVELOPMENT:
youthful | some age | aged

AROMAS:

DRY/SWEET:
bone dry | dry | off dry | medium sweet | sweet | very sweet

BODY:
very light | light | medium | medium-full | full-bodied | heavy

ACIDITY:
tart | crisp | lively | smooth | flabby

TANNINS (IF PRESENT):
LEVEL: low | medium | high   TYPE: soft | round | dry | hard

FLAVOUR INTENSITY:
low | moderate | flavourful | powerful

FLAVOURS: ˙

FINISH:
short (< 3 sec) | medium (4-5) | long (5-7) | v. long (>8 sec)

CONCLUSION/BALANCE:

rating:

FOOD: ## FOOD PAIRING:
MATCH: perfect | good | neutral | bad

tasting date: location:

tasting partner(s):

wine name:

producer:

region/appellation:

grape varieties:

vintage: alcohol: price:

COLOUR HUE:

WHITE: greenish | yellow | straw yellow | gold | amber
RED: purple | ruby | red | garnet | brick | brown
ROSÉ: pink | salmon | orange | copper

COLOUR DEPTH:
watery | pale | medium | deep | dark

CLARITY:
clear | slight haze | cloudy

AROMA INTENSITY:
low | moderate | aromatic | powerful

DEVELOPMENT:
youthful | some age | aged

AROMAS:

DRY/SWEET:
bone dry | dry | off dry | medium sweet | sweet | very sweet

BODY:
very light | light | medium | medium-full | full-bodied | heavy

ACIDITY:
tart | crisp | lively | smooth | flabby

TANNINS (IF PRESENT):
LEVEL: low | medium | high   TYPE: soft | round | dry | hard

FLAVOUR INTENSITY:
low | moderate | flavourful | powerful

FLAVOURS:

FINISH:
short (< 3 sec) | medium (4-5) | long (5-7) | v. long (>8 sec)

CONCLUSION/BALANCE:

rating:

FOOD: **FOOD PAIRING:**

MATCH: perfect | good | neutral | bad

tasting date: location:

tasting partner(s):

wine name:

producer:

region/appellation:

grape varieties:

vintage: alcohol: price:

COLOUR HUE:
WHITE: greenish | yellow | straw yellow | gold | amber
RED: purple | ruby | red | garnet | brick | brown
ROSÉ: pink | salmon | orange | copper

COLOUR DEPTH:
watery | pale | medium | deep | dark

CLARITY:
clear | slight haze | cloudy

AROMA INTENSITY:
low | moderate | aromatic | powerful

DEVELOPMENT:
youthful | some age | aged

AROMAS:

DRY/SWEET:
bone dry | dry | off dry | medium sweet | sweet | very sweet

BODY:
very light | light | medium | medium-full | full-bodied | heavy

ACIDITY:
tart | crisp | lively | smooth | flabby

TANNINS (IF PRESENT):
LEVEL: low | medium | high   TYPE: soft | round | dry | hard

FLAVOUR INTENSITY:
low | moderate | flavourful | powerful

FLAVOURS:

FINISH:
short (< 3 sec) | medium (4-5) | long (5-7) | v. long (>8 sec)

CONCLUSION/BALANCE:

rating:

FOOD: **FOOD PAIRING:**
MATCH: perfect | good | neutral | bad

tasting date: location:

tasting partner(s):

wine name:

producer:

region/appellation:

grape varieties:

vintage: alcohol: price:

COLOUR HUE:
WHITE: greenish | yellow | straw yellow | gold | amber
RED: purple | ruby | red | garnet | brick | brown
ROSÉ: pink | salmon | orange | copper

COLOUR DEPTH:
watery | pale | medium | deep | dark

CLARITY:
clear | slight haze | cloudy

AROMA INTENSITY:
low | moderate | aromatic | powerful

DEVELOPMENT:
youthful | some age | aged

AROMAS:

DRY/SWEET:
bone dry | dry | off dry | medium sweet | sweet | very sweet

BODY:
very light | light | medium | medium-full | full-bodied | heavy

ACIDITY:
tart | crisp | lively | smooth | flabby

TANNINS (IF PRESENT):
LEVEL: low | medium | high   TYPE: soft | round | dry | hard

FLAVOUR INTENSITY:
low | moderate | flavourful | powerful

FLAVOURS:

FINISH:
short (< 3 sec) | medium (4-5) | long (5-7) | v. long (>8 sec)

CONCLUSION/BALANCE:

rating:

FOOD: **FOOD PAIRING:**
                    MATCH: perfect | good | neutral | bad

tasting date: location:

tasting partner(s):

wine name:

producer:

region/appellation:

grape varieties:

vintage: alcohol: price:

COLOUR HUE:

WHITE: greenish | yellow | straw yellow | gold | amber
RED: purple | ruby | red | garnet | brick | brown
ROSÉ: pink | salmon | orange | copper

COLOUR DEPTH:
watery | pale | medium | deep | dark

CLARITY:
clear | slight haze | cloudy

AROMA INTENSITY:
low | moderate | aromatic | powerful

DEVELOPMENT:
youthful | some age | aged

AROMAS:

DRY/SWEET:
bone dry | dry | off dry | medium sweet | sweet | very sweet

BODY:
very light | light | medium | medium-full | full-bodied | heavy

ACIDITY:
tart | crisp | lively | smooth | flabby

TANNINS (IF PRESENT):
LEVEL: low | medium | high   TYPE: soft | round | dry | hard

FLAVOUR INTENSITY:
low | moderate | flavourful | powerful

FLAVOURS:

FINISH:
short (< 3 sec) | medium (4-5) | long (5-7) | v. long (>8 sec)

CONCLUSION/BALANCE:

rating:

FOOD: **FOOD PAIRING:**
                    MATCH: perfect | good | neutral | bad

tasting date: location:

tasting partner(s):

wine name:

producer:

region/appellation:

grape varieties:

vintage: alcohol: price:

COLOUR HUE:

WHITE: greenish | yellow | straw yellow | gold | amber
RED: purple | ruby | red | garnet | brick | brown
ROSÉ: pink | salmon | orange | copper

COLOUR DEPTH:
watery | pale | medium | deep | dark

CLARITY:
clear | slight haze | cloudy

AROMA INTENSITY:
low | moderate | aromatic | powerful

DEVELOPMENT:
youthful | some age | aged

AROMAS:

DRY/SWEET:
bone dry | dry | off dry | medium sweet | sweet | very sweet

BODY:
very light | light | medium | medium-full | full-bodied | heavy

ACIDITY:
tart | crisp | lively | smooth | flabby

TANNINS (IF PRESENT):
LEVEL: low | medium | high   TYPE: soft | round | dry | hard

FLAVOUR INTENSITY:
low | moderate | flavourful | powerful

FLAVOURS:

FINISH:
short (< 3 sec) | medium (4-5) | long (5-7) | v. long (>8 sec)

CONCLUSION/BALANCE:

rating:

FOOD: **FOOD PAIRING:**

MATCH: perfect | good | neutral | bad

tasting date: location:

tasting partner(s):

wine name:

producer:

region/appellation:

grape varieties:

vintage: alcohol: price:

COLOUR HUE:
WHITE: greenish | yellow | straw yellow | gold | amber
RED: purple | ruby | red | garnet | brick | brown
ROSÉ: pink | salmon | orange | copper

COLOUR DEPTH:
watery | pale | medium | deep | dark

CLARITY:
clear | slight haze | cloudy

AROMA INTENSITY:
low | moderate | aromatic | powerful

DEVELOPMENT:
youthful | some age | aged

AROMAS:

DRY/SWEET:
bone dry | dry | off dry | medium sweet | sweet | very sweet

BODY:
very light | light | medium | medium-full | full-bodied | heavy

ACIDITY:
tart | crisp | lively | smooth | flabby

TANNINS (IF PRESENT):
LEVEL: low | medium | high   TYPE: soft | round | dry | hard

FLAVOUR INTENSITY:
low | moderate | flavourful | powerful

FLAVOURS:

FINISH:
short (< 3 sec) | medium (4-5) | long (5-7) | v. long (>8 sec)

CONCLUSION/BALANCE:

rating:

FOOD: **FOOD PAIRING:**

MATCH: perfect | good | neutral | bad

tasting date: location:

tasting partner(s):

wine name:

producer:

region/appellation:

grape varieties:

vintage: alcohol: price:

COLOUR HUE:

WHITE: greenish | yellow | straw yellow | gold | amber
RED: purple | ruby | red | garnet | brick | brown
ROSÉ: pink | salmon | orange | copper

COLOUR DEPTH:
watery | pale | medium | deep | dark

CLARITY:
clear | slight haze | cloudy

AROMA INTENSITY:
low | moderate | aromatic | powerful

DEVELOPMENT:
youthful | some age | aged

AROMAS:

DRY/SWEET:
bone dry | dry | off dry | medium sweet | sweet | very sweet

BODY:
very light | light | medium | medium-full | full-bodied | heavy

ACIDITY:
tart | crisp | lively | smooth | flabby

TANNINS (IF PRESENT):
LEVEL: low | medium | high   TYPE: soft | round | dry | hard

FLAVOUR INTENSITY:
low | moderate | flavourful | powerful

FLAVOURS:

FINISH:
short (< 3 sec) | medium (4-5) | long (5-7) | v. long (>8 sec)

CONCLUSION/BALANCE:

rating:

FOOD: **FOOD PAIRING:**

MATCH: perfect | good | neutral | bad

tasting date: location:

tasting partner(s):

wine name:

producer:

region/appellation:

grape varieties:

vintage: alcohol: price:

COLOUR HUE:
WHITE: greenish | yellow | straw yellow | gold | amber
RED: purple | ruby | red | garnet | brick | brown
ROSÉ: pink | salmon | orange | copper

COLOUR DEPTH:
watery | pale | medium | deep | dark

CLARITY:
clear | slight haze | cloudy

AROMA INTENSITY:
low | moderate | aromatic | powerful

DEVELOPMENT:
youthful | some age | aged

AROMAS:

DRY/SWEET:
bone dry | dry | off dry | medium sweet | sweet | very sweet

BODY:
very light | light | medium | medium-full | full-bodied | heavy

ACIDITY:
tart | crisp | lively | smooth | flabby

TANNINS (IF PRESENT):
LEVEL: low | medium | high   TYPE: soft | round | dry | hard

FLAVOUR INTENSITY:
low | moderate | flavourful | powerful

FLAVOURS:

FINISH:
short (< 3 sec) | medium (4-5) | long (5-7) | v. long (>8 sec)

CONCLUSION/BALANCE:

rating:

FOOD: **FOOD PAIRING:**
                   MATCH: perfect | good | neutral | bad

tasting date: location:

tasting partner(s):

wine name:

producer:

region/appellation:

grape varieties:

vintage: alcohol: price:

COLOUR HUE:

 WHITE: greenish | yellow | straw yellow | gold | amber
RED: purple | ruby | red | garnet | brick | brown
ROSÉ: pink | salmon | orange | copper

COLOUR DEPTH:
watery | pale | medium | deep | dark

CLARITY:
clear | slight haze | cloudy

AROMA INTENSITY:
low | moderate | aromatic | powerful

DEVELOPMENT:
youthful | some age | aged

AROMAS:

DRY/SWEET:
bone dry | dry | off dry | medium sweet | sweet | very sweet

BODY:
very light | light | medium | medium-full | full-bodied | heavy

ACIDITY:
tart | crisp | lively | smooth | flabby

TANNINS (IF PRESENT):
LEVEL: low | medium | high   TYPE: soft | round | dry | hard

FLAVOUR INTENSITY:
low | moderate | flavourful | powerful

FLAVOURS:

FINISH:
short (< 3 sec) | medium (4-5) | long (5-7) | v. long (>8 sec)

CONCLUSION/BALANCE:

rating:

FOOD: **FOOD PAIRING:**

MATCH: perfect | good | neutral | bad

tasting date: location:

tasting partner(s):

wine name:

producer:

region/appellation:

grape varieties:

vintage: alcohol: price:

COLOUR HUE:

WHITE: greenish | yellow | straw yellow | gold | amber
RED: purple | ruby | red | garnet | brick | brown
ROSÉ: pink | salmon | orange | copper

COLOUR DEPTH:
watery | pale | medium | deep | dark

CLARITY:
clear | slight haze | cloudy

AROMA INTENSITY:
low | moderate | aromatic | powerful

DEVELOPMENT:
youthful | some age | aged

AROMAS:

DRY/SWEET:
bone dry | dry | off dry | medium sweet | sweet | very sweet

BODY:
very light | light | medium | medium-full | full-bodied | heavy

ACIDITY:
tart | crisp | lively | smooth | flabby

TANNINS (IF PRESENT):
LEVEL: low | medium | high   TYPE: soft | round | dry | hard

FLAVOUR INTENSITY:
low | moderate | flavourful | powerful

FLAVOURS:

FINISH:
short (< 3 sec) | medium (4-5) | long (5-7) | v. long (>8 sec)

CONCLUSION/BALANCE:

rating:

FOOD: **FOOD PAIRING:**
                 MATCH: perfect | good | neutral | bad

tasting date: location:

tasting partner(s):

wine name:

producer:

region/appellation:

grape varieties:

vintage: alcohol: price:

COLOUR HUE:
WHITE: greenish | yellow | straw yellow | gold | amber
RED: purple | ruby | red | garnet | brick | brown
ROSÉ: pink | salmon | orange | copper

COLOUR DEPTH:
watery | pale | medium | deep | dark

CLARITY:
clear | slight haze | cloudy

AROMA INTENSITY:
low | moderate | aromatic | powerful

DEVELOPMENT:
youthful | some age | aged

AROMAS:

DRY/SWEET:
bone dry | dry | off dry | medium sweet | sweet | very sweet

BODY:
very light | light | medium | medium-full | full-bodied | heavy

ACIDITY:
tart | crisp | lively | smooth | flabby

TANNINS (IF PRESENT):
LEVEL: low | medium | high   TYPE: soft | round | dry | hard

FLAVOUR INTENSITY:
low | moderate | flavourful | powerful

FLAVOURS:

FINISH:
short (< 3 sec) | medium (4-5) | long (5-7) | v. long (>8 sec)

CONCLUSION/BALANCE:

rating:

FOOD: **FOOD PAIRING:**

MATCH: perfect | good | neutral | bad

tasting date: location:

tasting partner(s):

wine name:

producer:

region/appellation:

grape varieties:

vintage: alcohol: price:

COLOUR HUE:

WHITE: greenish | yellow | straw yellow | gold | amber
RED: purple | ruby | red | garnet | brick | brown
ROSÉ: pink | salmon | orange | copper

COLOUR DEPTH:
watery | pale | medium | deep | dark

CLARITY:
clear | slight haze | cloudy

AROMA INTENSITY:
low | moderate | aromatic | powerful

DEVELOPMENT:
youthful | some age | aged

AROMAS:

DRY/SWEET:
bone dry | dry | off dry | medium sweet | sweet | very sweet

BODY:
very light | light | medium | medium-full | full-bodied | heavy

ACIDITY:
tart | crisp | lively | smooth | flabby

TANNINS (IF PRESENT):
LEVEL: low | medium | high   TYPE: soft | round | dry | hard

FLAVOUR INTENSITY:
low | moderate | flavourful | powerful

FLAVOURS:

FINISH:
short (< 3 sec) | medium (4-5) | long (5-7) | v. long (>8 sec)

CONCLUSION/BALANCE:

rating:

FOOD: **FOOD PAIRING:**

MATCH: perfect | good | neutral | bad

tasting date: location:

tasting partner(s):

wine name:

producer:

region/appellation:

grape varieties:

vintage: alcohol: price:

COLOUR HUE:

WHITE: greenish | yellow | straw yellow | gold | amber
RED: purple | ruby | red | garnet | brick | brown
ROSÉ: pink | salmon | orange | copper

COLOUR DEPTH:
watery | pale | medium | deep | dark

CLARITY:
clear | slight haze | cloudy

AROMA INTENSITY:
low | moderate | aromatic | powerful

DEVELOPMENT:
youthful | some age | aged

AROMAS:

DRY/SWEET:
bone dry | dry | off dry | medium sweet | sweet | very sweet

BODY:
very light | light | medium | medium-full | full-bodied | heavy

ACIDITY:
tart | crisp | lively | smooth | flabby

TANNINS (IF PRESENT):
LEVEL: low | medium | high   TYPE: soft | round | dry | hard

FLAVOUR INTENSITY:
low | moderate | flavourful | powerful

FLAVOURS:

FINISH:
short (< 3 sec) | medium (4-5) | long (5-7) | v. long (>8 sec)

CONCLUSION/BALANCE:

rating:

FOOD: **FOOD PAIRING:**

MATCH: perfect | good | neutral | bad

tasting date: location:

tasting partner(s):

wine name:

producer:

region/appellation:

grape varieties:

vintage: alcohol: price:

COLOUR HUE:
WHITE: greenish | yellow | straw yellow | gold | amber
RED: purple | ruby | red | garnet | brick | brown
ROSÉ: pink | salmon | orange | copper

COLOUR DEPTH:
watery | pale | medium | deep | dark

CLARITY:
clear | slight haze | cloudy

AROMA INTENSITY:
low | moderate | aromatic | powerful

DEVELOPMENT:
youthful | some age | aged

AROMAS:

DRY/SWEET:
bone dry | dry | off dry | medium sweet | sweet | very sweet

BODY:
very light | light | medium | medium-full | full-bodied | heavy

ACIDITY:
tart | crisp | lively | smooth | flabby

TANNINS (IF PRESENT):
LEVEL: low | medium | high   TYPE: soft | round | dry | hard

FLAVOUR INTENSITY:
low | moderate | flavourful | powerful

FLAVOURS:

FINISH:
short (< 3 sec) | medium (4-5) | long (5-7) | v. long (>8 sec)

CONCLUSION/BALANCE:

rating:

FOOD: **FOOD PAIRING:**
                    MATCH: perfect | good | neutral | bad

tasting date: location:

tasting partner(s):

wine name:

producer:

region/appellation:

grape varieties:

vintage: alcohol: price:

COLOUR HUE:
WHITE: greenish | yellow | straw yellow | gold | amber
RED: purple | ruby | red | garnet | brick | brown
ROSÉ: pink | salmon | orange | copper

COLOUR DEPTH:
watery | pale | medium | deep | dark

CLARITY:
clear | slight haze | cloudy

AROMA INTENSITY:
low | moderate | aromatic | powerful

DEVELOPMENT:
youthful | some age | aged

AROMAS:

DRY/SWEET:
bone dry | dry | off dry | medium sweet | sweet | very sweet

BODY:
very light | light | medium | medium-full | full-bodied | heavy

ACIDITY:
tart | crisp | lively | smooth | flabby

TANNINS (IF PRESENT):
LEVEL: low | medium | high   TYPE: soft | round | dry | hard

FLAVOUR INTENSITY:
low | moderate | flavourful | powerful

FLAVOURS:

FINISH:
short (< 3 sec) | medium (4-5) | long (5-7) | v. long (>8 sec)

CONCLUSION/BALANCE:

rating:

FOOD: **FOOD PAIRING:**
                    MATCH: perfect | good | neutral | bad

tasting date: location:

tasting partner(s):

wine name:

producer:

region/appellation:

grape varieties:

vintage: alcohol: price:

COLOUR HUE:
WHITE: greenish | yellow | straw yellow | gold | amber
RED: purple | ruby | red | garnet | brick | brown
ROSÉ: pink | salmon | orange | copper

COLOUR DEPTH:
watery | pale | medium | deep | dark

CLARITY:
clear | slight haze | cloudy

AROMA INTENSITY:
low | moderate | aromatic | powerful

DEVELOPMENT:
youthful | some age | aged

AROMAS:

DRY/SWEET:
bone dry | dry | off dry | medium sweet | sweet | very sweet

BODY:
very light | light | medium | medium-full | full-bodied | heavy

ACIDITY:
tart | crisp | lively | smooth | flabby

TANNINS (IF PRESENT):
LEVEL: low | medium | high   TYPE: soft | round | dry | hard

FLAVOUR INTENSITY:
low | moderate | flavourful | powerful

FLAVOURS:

FINISH:
short (< 3 sec) | medium (4-5) | long (5-7) | v. long (>8 sec)

CONCLUSION/BALANCE:

rating:

FOOD: **FOOD PAIRING:**
                 MATCH: perfect | good | neutral | bad

tasting date: location:

tasting partner(s):

wine name:

producer:

region/appellation:

grape varieties:

vintage: alcohol: price:

COLOUR HUE:

WHITE: greenish | yellow | straw yellow | gold | amber
RED: purple | ruby | red | garnet | brick | brown
ROSÉ: pink | salmon | orange | copper

COLOUR DEPTH:
watery | pale | medium | deep | dark

CLARITY:
clear | slight haze | cloudy

AROMA INTENSITY:
low | moderate | aromatic | powerful

DEVELOPMENT:
youthful | some age | aged

AROMAS:

DRY/SWEET:
bone dry | dry | off dry | medium sweet | sweet | very sweet

BODY:
very light | light | medium | medium-full | full-bodied | heavy

ACIDITY:
tart | crisp | lively | smooth | flabby

TANNINS (IF PRESENT):
LEVEL: low | medium | high   TYPE: soft | round | dry | hard

FLAVOUR INTENSITY:
low | moderate | flavourful | powerful

FLAVOURS:

FINISH:
short (< 3 sec) | medium (4-5) | long (5-7) | v. long (>8 sec)

CONCLUSION/BALANCE:

rating:

FOOD: **FOOD PAIRING:**

MATCH: perfect | good | neutral | bad

tasting date: location:

tasting partner(s):

wine name:

producer:

region/appellation:

grape varieties:

vintage: alcohol: price:

COLOUR HUE:

WHITE: greenish | yellow | straw yellow | gold | amber
RED: purple | ruby | red | garnet | brick | brown
ROSÉ: pink | salmon | orange | copper

COLOUR DEPTH:
watery | pale | medium | deep | dark

CLARITY:
clear | slight haze | cloudy

AROMA INTENSITY:
low | moderate | aromatic | powerful

DEVELOPMENT:
youthful | some age | aged

AROMAS:

DRY/SWEET:
bone dry | dry | off dry | medium sweet | sweet | very sweet

BODY:
very light | light | medium | medium-full | full-bodied | heavy

ACIDITY:
tart | crisp | lively | smooth | flabby

TANNINS (IF PRESENT):
LEVEL: low | medium | high   TYPE: soft | round | dry | hard

FLAVOUR INTENSITY:
low | moderate | flavourful | powerful

FLAVOURS:

FINISH:
short (< 3 sec) | medium (4-5) | long (5-7) | v. long (>8 sec)

CONCLUSION/BALANCE:

rating:

FOOD: **FOOD PAIRING:**
                    MATCH: perfect | good | neutral | bad

tasting date: location:

tasting partner(s):

wine name:

producer:

region/appellation:

grape varieties:

vintage: alcohol: price:

COLOUR HUE:
WHITE: greenish | yellow | straw yellow | gold | amber
RED: purple | ruby | red | garnet | brick | brown
ROSÉ: pink | salmon | orange | copper

COLOUR DEPTH:
watery | pale | medium | deep | dark

CLARITY:
clear | slight haze | cloudy

AROMA INTENSITY:
low | moderate | aromatic | powerful

DEVELOPMENT:
youthful | some age | aged

AROMAS:

DRY/SWEET:
bone dry | dry | off dry | medium sweet | sweet | very sweet

BODY:
very light | light | medium | medium-full | full-bodied | heavy

ACIDITY:
tart | crisp | lively | smooth | flabby

TANNINS (IF PRESENT):
LEVEL: low | medium | high TYPE: soft | round | dry | hard

FLAVOUR INTENSITY:
low | moderate | flavourful | powerful

FLAVOURS:

FINISH:
short (< 3 sec) | medium (4-5) | long (5-7) | v. long (>8 sec)

CONCLUSION/BALANCE:

rating:

FOOD: **FOOD PAIRING:**

MATCH: perfect | good | neutral | bad

tasting date: location:

tasting partner(s):

wine name:

producer:

region/appellation:

grape varieties:

vintage: alcohol: price:

COLOUR HUE:
WHITE: greenish | yellow | straw yellow | gold | amber
RED: purple | ruby | red | garnet | brick | brown
ROSÉ: pink | salmon | orange | copper

COLOUR DEPTH:
watery | pale | medium | deep | dark

CLARITY:
clear | slight haze | cloudy

AROMA INTENSITY:
low | moderate | aromatic | powerful

DEVELOPMENT:
youthful | some age | aged

AROMAS:

DRY/SWEET:
bone dry | dry | off dry | medium sweet | sweet | very sweet

BODY:
very light | light | medium | medium-full | full-bodied | heavy

ACIDITY:
tart | crisp | lively | smooth | flabby

TANNINS (IF PRESENT):
LEVEL: low | medium | high   TYPE: soft | round | dry | hard

FLAVOUR INTENSITY:
low | moderate | flavourful | powerful

FLAVOURS:

FINISH:
short (< 3 sec) | medium (4-5) | long (5-7) | v. long (>8 sec)

CONCLUSION/BALANCE:

rating:

FOOD: **FOOD PAIRING:**
                MATCH: perfect | good | neutral | bad

tasting date:

location:

tasting partner(s):

wine name:

producer:

region/appellation:

grape varieties:

vintage:

alcohol:

price:

COLOUR HUE:

WHITE: greenish | yellow | straw yellow | gold | amber
RED: purple | ruby | red | garnet | brick | brown
ROSÉ: pink | salmon | orange | copper

COLOUR DEPTH:
watery | pale | medium | deep | dark

CLARITY:
clear | slight haze | cloudy

AROMA INTENSITY:
low | moderate | aromatic | powerful

DEVELOPMENT:
youthful | some age | aged

AROMAS:

DRY/SWEET:
bone dry | dry | off dry | medium sweet | sweet | very sweet

BODY:
very light | light | medium | medium-full | full-bodied | heavy

ACIDITY:
tart | crisp | lively | smooth | flabby

TANNINS (IF PRESENT):
LEVEL: low | medium | high   TYPE: soft | round | dry | hard

FLAVOUR INTENSITY:
low | moderate | flavourful | powerful

FLAVOURS:

FINISH:
short (< 3 sec) | medium (4-5) | long (5-7) | v. long (>8 sec)

CONCLUSION/BALANCE:

rating:

FOOD:

FOOD PAIRING:

MATCH: perfect | good | neutral | bad

tasting date: location:

tasting partner(s):

wine name:

producer:

region/appellation:

grape varieties:

vintage: alcohol: price:

COLOUR HUE:

WHITE: greenish | yellow | straw yellow | gold | amber
RED: purple | ruby | red | garnet | brick | brown
ROSÉ: pink | salmon | orange | copper

COLOUR DEPTH:
watery | pale | medium | deep | dark

CLARITY:
clear | slight haze | cloudy

AROMA INTENSITY:
low | moderate | aromatic | powerful

DEVELOPMENT:
youthful | some age | aged

AROMAS:

DRY/SWEET:
bone dry | dry | off dry | medium sweet | sweet | very sweet

BODY:
very light | light | medium | medium-full | full-bodied | heavy

ACIDITY:
tart | crisp | lively | smooth | flabby

TANNINS (IF PRESENT):
LEVEL: low | medium | high   TYPE: soft | round | dry | hard

FLAVOUR INTENSITY:
low | moderate | flavourful | powerful

FLAVOURS:

FINISH:
short (< 3 sec) | medium (4-5) | long (5-7) | v. long (>8 sec)

CONCLUSION/BALANCE:

rating:

FOOD: **FOOD PAIRING:**
               MATCH: perfect | good | neutral | bad

tasting date: location:

tasting partner(s):

wine name:

producer:

region/appellation:

grape varieties:

vintage: alcohol: price:

COLOUR HUE:
WHITE: greenish | yellow | straw yellow | gold | amber
RED: purple | ruby | red | garnet | brick | brown
ROSÉ: pink | salmon | orange | copper

COLOUR DEPTH:
watery | pale | medium | deep | dark

CLARITY:
clear | slight haze | cloudy

AROMA INTENSITY:
low | moderate | aromatic | powerful

DEVELOPMENT:
youthful | some age | aged

AROMAS:

DRY/SWEET:
bone dry | dry | off dry | medium sweet | sweet | very sweet

BODY:
very light | light | medium | medium-full | full-bodied | heavy

ACIDITY:
tart | crisp | lively | smooth | flabby

TANNINS (IF PRESENT):
LEVEL: low | medium | high   TYPE: soft | round | dry | hard

FLAVOUR INTENSITY:
low | moderate | flavourful | powerful

FLAVOURS:

FINISH:
short (< 3 sec) | medium (4-5) | long (5-7) | v. long (>8 sec)

CONCLUSION/BALANCE:

rating:

FOOD: **FOOD PAIRING:**

MATCH: perfect | good | neutral | bad

tasting date: location:

tasting partner(s):

wine name:

producer:

region/appellation:

grape varieties:

vintage: alcohol: price:

COLOUR HUE:

WHITE: greenish | yellow | straw yellow | gold | amber
RED: purple | ruby | red | garnet | brick | brown
ROSÉ: pink | salmon | orange | copper

COLOUR DEPTH:
watery | pale | medium | deep | dark

CLARITY:
clear | slight haze | cloudy

AROMA INTENSITY:
low | moderate | aromatic | powerful

DEVELOPMENT:
youthful | some age | aged

AROMAS:

DRY/SWEET:
bone dry | dry | off dry | medium sweet | sweet | very sweet

BODY:
very light | light | medium | medium-full | full-bodied | heavy

ACIDITY:
tart | crisp | lively | smooth | flabby

TANNINS (IF PRESENT):
LEVEL: low | medium | high   TYPE: soft | round | dry | hard

FLAVOUR INTENSITY:
low | moderate | flavourful | powerful

FLAVOURS:

FINISH:
short (< 3 sec) | medium (4-5) | long (5-7) | v. long (>8 sec)

CONCLUSION/BALANCE:

rating:

FOOD: **FOOD PAIRING:**

MATCH: perfect | good | neutral | bad

tasting date: location:

tasting partner(s):

wine name:

producer:

region/appellation:

grape varieties:

vintage: alcohol: price:

COLOUR HUE:
WHITE: greenish | yellow | straw yellow | gold | amber
RED: purple | ruby | red | garnet | brick | brown
ROSÉ: pink | salmon | orange | copper

COLOUR DEPTH:
watery | pale | medium | deep | dark

CLARITY:
clear | slight haze | cloudy

AROMA INTENSITY:
low | moderate | aromatic | powerful

DEVELOPMENT:
youthful | some age | aged

AROMAS:

DRY/SWEET:
bone dry | dry | off dry | medium sweet | sweet | very sweet

BODY:
very light | light | medium | medium-full | full-bodied | heavy

ACIDITY:
tart | crisp | lively | smooth | flabby

TANNINS (IF PRESENT):
LEVEL: low | medium | high   TYPE: soft | round | dry | hard

FLAVOUR INTENSITY:
low | moderate | flavourful | powerful

FLAVOURS:

FINISH:
short (< 3 sec) | medium (4-5) | long (5-7) | v. long (>8 sec)

CONCLUSION/BALANCE:

rating:

FOOD: **FOOD PAIRING:**

MATCH: perfect | good | neutral | bad

tasting date: location:

tasting partner(s):

wine name:

producer:

region/appellation:

grape varieties:

vintage: alcohol: price:

COLOUR HUE:
WHITE: greenish | yellow | straw yellow | gold | amber
RED: purple | ruby | red | garnet | brick | brown
ROSÉ: pink | salmon | orange | copper

COLOUR DEPTH:
watery | pale | medium | deep | dark

CLARITY:
clear | slight haze | cloudy

AROMA INTENSITY:
low | moderate | aromatic | powerful

DEVELOPMENT:
youthful | some age | aged

AROMAS:

DRY/SWEET:
bone dry | dry | off dry | medium sweet | sweet | very sweet

BODY:
very light | light | medium | medium-full | full-bodied | heavy

ACIDITY:
tart | crisp | lively | smooth | flabby

TANNINS (IF PRESENT):
LEVEL: low | medium | high   TYPE: soft | round | dry | hard

FLAVOUR INTENSITY:
low | moderate | flavourful | powerful

FLAVOURS:

FINISH:
short (< 3 sec) | medium (4-5) | long (5-7) | v. long (>8 sec)

CONCLUSION/BALANCE:

rating:

FOOD: **FOOD PAIRING:**
                        MATCH: perfect | good | neutral | bad

tasting date: location:

tasting partner(s):

wine name:

producer:

region/appellation:

grape varieties:

vintage: alcohol: price:

COLOUR HUE:
WHITE: greenish | yellow | straw yellow | gold | amber
RED: purple | ruby | red | garnet | brick | brown
ROSÉ: pink | salmon | orange | copper

COLOUR DEPTH:
watery | pale | medium | deep | dark

CLARITY:
clear | slight haze | cloudy

AROMA INTENSITY:
low | moderate | aromatic | powerful

DEVELOPMENT:
youthful | some age | aged

AROMAS:

DRY/SWEET:
bone dry | dry | off dry | medium sweet | sweet | very sweet

BODY:
very light | light | medium | medium-full | full-bodied | heavy

ACIDITY:
tart | crisp | lively | smooth | flabby

TANNINS (IF PRESENT):
LEVEL: low | medium | high   TYPE: soft | round | dry | hard

FLAVOUR INTENSITY:
low | moderate | flavourful | powerful

FLAVOURS:

FINISH:
short (< 3 sec) | medium (4-5) | long (5-7) | v. long (>8 sec)

CONCLUSION/BALANCE:

rating:

FOOD: **FOOD PAIRING:**
                 MATCH: perfect | good | neutral | bad

tasting date: location:

tasting partner(s):

wine name:

producer:

region/appellation:

grape varieties:

vintage: alcohol: price:

COLOUR HUE:

WHITE: greenish | yellow | straw yellow | gold | amber
RED: purple | ruby | red | garnet | brick | brown
ROSÉ: pink | salmon | orange | copper

COLOUR DEPTH:
watery | pale | medium | deep | dark

CLARITY:
clear | slight haze | cloudy

AROMA INTENSITY:
low | moderate | aromatic | powerful

DEVELOPMENT:
youthful | some age | aged

AROMAS:

DRY/SWEET:
bone dry | dry | off dry | medium sweet | sweet | very sweet

BODY:
very light | light | medium | medium-full | full-bodied | heavy

ACIDITY:
tart | crisp | lively | smooth | flabby

TANNINS (IF PRESENT):
LEVEL: low | medium | high   TYPE: soft | round | dry | hard

FLAVOUR INTENSITY:
low | moderate | flavourful | powerful

FLAVOURS:

FINISH:
short (< 3 sec) | medium (4-5) | long (5-7) | v. long (>8 sec)

CONCLUSION/BALANCE:

rating:

FOOD: **FOOD PAIRING:**
                    MATCH: perfect | good | neutral | bad

tasting date: location:

tasting partner(s):

wine name:

producer:

region/appellation:

grape varieties:

vintage: alcohol: price:

COLOUR HUE:
WHITE: greenish | yellow | straw yellow | gold | amber
RED: purple | ruby | red | garnet | brick | brown
ROSÉ: pink | salmon | orange | copper

COLOUR DEPTH:
watery | pale | medium | deep | dark

CLARITY:
clear | slight haze | cloudy

AROMA INTENSITY:
low | moderate | aromatic | powerful

DEVELOPMENT:
youthful | some age | aged

AROMAS:

DRY/SWEET:
bone dry | dry | off dry | medium sweet | sweet | very sweet

BODY:
very light | light | medium | medium-full | full-bodied | heavy

ACIDITY:
tart | crisp | lively | smooth | flabby

TANNINS (IF PRESENT):
LEVEL: low | medium | high   TYPE: soft | round | dry | hard

FLAVOUR INTENSITY:
low | moderate | flavourful | powerful

FLAVOURS:

FINISH:
short (< 3 sec) | medium (4-5) | long (5-7) | v. long (>8 sec)

CONCLUSION/BALANCE:

rating:

FOOD: **FOOD PAIRING:**

MATCH: perfect | good | neutral | bad

tasting date: location:

tasting partner(s):

wine name:

producer:

region/appellation:

grape varieties:

vintage: alcohol: price:

COLOUR HUE:

WHITE: greenish | yellow | straw yellow | gold | amber
RED: purple | ruby | red | garnet | brick | brown
ROSÉ: pink | salmon | orange | copper

COLOUR DEPTH:
watery | pale | medium | deep | dark

CLARITY:
clear | slight haze | cloudy

AROMA INTENSITY:
low | moderate | aromatic | powerful

DEVELOPMENT:
youthful | some age | aged

AROMAS:

DRY/SWEET:
bone dry | dry | off dry | medium sweet | sweet | very sweet

BODY:
very light | light | medium | medium-full | full-bodied | heavy

ACIDITY:
tart | crisp | lively | smooth | flabby

TANNINS (IF PRESENT):
LEVEL: low | medium | high   TYPE: soft | round | dry | hard

FLAVOUR INTENSITY:
low | moderate | flavourful | powerful

FLAVOURS:

FINISH:
short (< 3 sec) | medium (4-5) | long (5-7) | v. long (>8 sec)

CONCLUSION/BALANCE:

rating:

FOOD: **FOOD PAIRING:**

MATCH: perfect | good | neutral | bad

tasting date: location:

tasting partner(s):

wine name:

producer:

region/appellation:

grape varieties:

vintage: alcohol: price:

COLOUR HUE:

WHITE: greenish | yellow | straw yellow | gold | amber
RED: purple | ruby | red | garnet | brick | brown
ROSÉ: pink | salmon | orange | copper

COLOUR DEPTH:
watery | pale | medium | deep | dark

CLARITY:
clear | slight haze | cloudy

AROMA INTENSITY:
low | moderate | aromatic | powerful

DEVELOPMENT:
youthful | some age | aged

AROMAS:

DRY/SWEET:
bone dry | dry | off dry | medium sweet | sweet | very sweet

BODY:
very light | light | medium | medium-full | full-bodied | heavy

ACIDITY:
tart | crisp | lively | smooth | flabby

TANNINS (IF PRESENT):
LEVEL: low | medium | high   TYPE: soft | round | dry | hard

FLAVOUR INTENSITY:
low | moderate | flavourful | powerful

FLAVOURS:

FINISH:
short (< 3 sec) | medium (4-5) | long (5-7) | v. long (>8 sec)

CONCLUSION/BALANCE:

rating:

FOOD: **FOOD PAIRING:**

MATCH: perfect | good | neutral | bad

tasting date: location:

tasting partner(s):

wine name:

producer:

region/appellation:

grape varieties:

vintage: alcohol: price:

COLOUR HUE:

WHITE: greenish | yellow | straw yellow | gold | amber
RED: purple | ruby | red | garnet | brick | brown
ROSÉ: pink | salmon | orange | copper

COLOUR DEPTH:

watery | pale | medium | deep | dark

CLARITY:

clear | slight haze | cloudy

AROMA INTENSITY:

low | moderate | aromatic | powerful

DEVELOPMENT:

youthful | some age | aged

AROMAS:

DRY/SWEET:

bone dry | dry | off dry | medium sweet | sweet | very sweet

BODY:

very light | light | medium | medium-full | full-bodied | heavy

ACIDITY:

tart | crisp | lively | smooth | flabby

TANNINS (IF PRESENT):

LEVEL: low | medium | high   TYPE: soft | round | dry | hard

FLAVOUR INTENSITY:

low | moderate | flavourful | powerful

FLAVOURS: ˙

FINISH:

short (< 3 sec) | medium (4-5) | long (5-7) | v. long (>8 sec)

CONCLUSION/BALANCE:

rating:

FOOD: **FOOD PAIRING:**

MATCH: perfect | good | neutral | bad

tasting date: location:

tasting partner(s):

wine name:

producer:

region/appellation:

grape varieties:

vintage: alcohol: price:

COLOUR HUE:
WHITE: greenish | yellow | straw yellow | gold | amber
RED: purple | ruby | red | garnet | brick | brown
ROSÉ: pink | salmon | orange | copper

COLOUR DEPTH:
watery | pale | medium | deep | dark

CLARITY:
clear | slight haze | cloudy

AROMA INTENSITY:
low | moderate | aromatic | powerful

DEVELOPMENT:
youthful | some age | aged

AROMAS:

DRY/SWEET:
bone dry | dry | off dry | medium sweet | sweet | very sweet

BODY:
very light | light | medium | medium-full | full-bodied | heavy

ACIDITY:
tart | crisp | lively | smooth | flabby

TANNINS (IF PRESENT):
LEVEL: low | medium | high   TYPE: soft | round | dry | hard

FLAVOUR INTENSITY:
low | moderate | flavourful | powerful

FLAVOURS:

FINISH:
short (< 3 sec) | medium (4-5) | long (5-7) | v. long (>8 sec)

CONCLUSION/BALANCE:

rating:

FOOD: **FOOD PAIRING:**

MATCH: perfect | good | neutral | bad

tasting date: location:

tasting partner(s):

wine name:

producer:

region/appellation:

grape varieties:

vintage: alcohol: price:

COLOUR HUE:
WHITE: greenish | yellow | straw yellow | gold | amber
RED: purple | ruby | red | garnet | brick | brown
ROSÉ: pink | salmon | orange | copper

COLOUR DEPTH:
watery | pale | medium | deep | dark

CLARITY:
clear | slight haze | cloudy

AROMA INTENSITY:
low | moderate | aromatic | powerful

DEVELOPMENT:
youthful | some age | aged

AROMAS:

DRY/SWEET:
bone dry | dry | off dry | medium sweet | sweet | very sweet

BODY:
very light | light | medium | medium-full | full-bodied | heavy

ACIDITY:
tart | crisp | lively | smooth | flabby

TANNINS (IF PRESENT):
LEVEL: low | medium | high   TYPE: soft | round | dry | hard

FLAVOUR INTENSITY:
low | moderate | flavourful | powerful

FLAVOURS:

FINISH:
short (< 3 sec) | medium (4-5) | long (5-7) | v. long (>8 sec)

CONCLUSION/BALANCE:

rating:

FOOD:

FOOD PAIRING:
MATCH: perfect | good | neutral | bad

tasting date: location:

tasting partner(s):

wine name:

producer:

region/appellation:

grape varieties:

vintage: alcohol: price:

COLOUR HUE:

WHITE: greenish | yellow | straw yellow | gold | amber
RED: purple | ruby | red | garnet | brick | brown
ROSÉ: pink | salmon | orange | copper

COLOUR DEPTH:
watery | pale | medium | deep | dark

CLARITY:
clear | slight haze | cloudy

AROMA INTENSITY:
low | moderate | aromatic | powerful

DEVELOPMENT:
youthful | some age | aged

AROMAS:

DRY/SWEET:
bone dry | dry | off dry | medium sweet | sweet | very sweet

BODY:
very light | light | medium | medium-full | full-bodied | heavy

ACIDITY:
tart | crisp | lively | smooth | flabby

TANNINS (IF PRESENT):
LEVEL: low | medium | high   TYPE: soft | round | dry | hard

FLAVOUR INTENSITY:
low | moderate | flavourful | powerful

FLAVOURS:

FINISH:
short (< 3 sec) | medium (4-5) | long (5-7) | v. long (>8 sec)

CONCLUSION/BALANCE:

rating:

FOOD: **FOOD PAIRING:**

MATCH: perfect | good | neutral | bad

tasting date: location:

tasting partner(s):

wine name:

producer:

region/appellation:

grape varieties:

vintage: alcohol: price:

COLOUR HUE:
WHITE: greenish | yellow | straw yellow | gold | amber
RED: purple | ruby | red | garnet | brick | brown
ROSÉ: pink | salmon | orange | copper

COLOUR DEPTH:
watery | pale | medium | deep | dark

CLARITY:
clear | slight haze | cloudy

AROMA INTENSITY:
low | moderate | aromatic | powerful

DEVELOPMENT:
youthful | some age | aged

AROMAS:

DRY/SWEET:
bone dry | dry | off dry | medium sweet | sweet | very sweet

BODY:
very light | light | medium | medium-full | full-bodied | heavy

ACIDITY:
tart | crisp | lively | smooth | flabby

TANNINS (IF PRESENT):
LEVEL: low | medium | high   TYPE: soft | round | dry | hard

FLAVOUR INTENSITY:
low | moderate | flavourful | powerful

FLAVOURS:

FINISH:
short (< 3 sec) | medium (4-5) | long (5-7) | v. long (>8 sec)

CONCLUSION/BALANCE:

rating:

FOOD: **FOOD PAIRING:**
                    MATCH: perfect | good | neutral | bad

tasting date: location:

tasting partner(s):

wine name:

producer:

region/appellation:

grape varieties:

vintage: alcohol: price:

COLOUR HUE:
WHITE: greenish | yellow | straw yellow | gold | amber
RED: purple | ruby | red | garnet | brick | brown
ROSÉ: pink | salmon | orange | copper

COLOUR DEPTH:
watery | pale | medium | deep | dark

CLARITY:
clear | slight haze | cloudy

AROMA INTENSITY:
low | moderate | aromatic | powerful

DEVELOPMENT:
youthful | some age | aged

AROMAS:

DRY/SWEET:
bone dry | dry | off dry | medium sweet | sweet | very sweet

BODY:
very light | light | medium | medium-full | full-bodied | heavy

ACIDITY:
tart | crisp | lively | smooth | flabby

TANNINS (IF PRESENT):
LEVEL: low | medium | high   TYPE: soft | round | dry | hard

FLAVOUR INTENSITY:
low | moderate | flavourful | powerful

FLAVOURS:

FINISH:
short (< 3 sec) | medium (4-5) | long (5-7) | v. long (>8 sec)

CONCLUSION/BALANCE:

rating:

FOOD: **FOOD PAIRING:**

                     MATCH: perfect | good | neutral | bad

WINE TASTING TERMS

Here are the most common wine tasting terms used today, along with examples of wines (indicated by *grape variety* and/or *region*) to which they frequently apply. Where necessary, a brief explanation of the term is given. Many of these characteristics or flavours can be found in a variety of wines – not just the few listed – so it helps to taste with an open mind.

The coloured boxes on this list are all AROMA DESCRIPTORS, with GENERAL TERMS and WINE FAULTS on the far right.

To better understand how these terms are used as part of a tasting note, please see HOW TO TAKE A WINE TASTING NOTE in the notebook.

FLORAL

Often described simply as FLORAL, these specific terms are commonly used as well.

ACACIA *Marsanne, Sauternes,* sparkling wine

CHERRY BLOSSOM

ELDERFLOWER underripe *Sauvignon Blanc*

LAVENDER *Southern Rhône, Australian Riesling*

LINDEN *Loire Chenin Blanc*

LINALOOL *Gewürztraminer*

ORANGE BLOSSOM *Muscat*

ROSE *Nebbiolo, Muscat Blanc, Gewürztraminer*

VIOLET *red Burgundy, red Bordeaux, Malbec, Mourvèdre, mature Petit Verdot*

WHITE FLOWERS

VEGETAL

VEGETAL aromas are desirable elements of some grape varieties but can be considered faults due to underripe grapes in others.

ASPARAGUS *New Zealand Sauvignon Blanc*

BEETROOT *red Burgundy*

GREEN (BELL) PEPPER *Cabernet Franc, Sauvignon Blanc, Cabernet Sauvignon*

BLACK OLIVE aged reds

CUCUMBER

GRASS *Sauvignon Blanc, Colombard*

GREEN OLIVE *Fino Sherry*

GREEN PEA

LENTIL *Grüner Veltliner*

HERBS & SPICES

Wines are often described as just SPICY or HERBAL when no single spice or herb applies.

ALLSPICE blend of CLOVE, BLACK PEPPER, CINNAMON and NUTMEG

ANISE, FENNEL, LICORICE *Cabernet Sauvignon, Grenache, Mourvèdre*

BASIL

BLACK PEPPER *Syrah*

CINNAMON

CLOVE *Sangiovese*

DILL

EUCALYPTUS NEW WORLD reds

GINGER

HORSERADISH *Pinot Noir*

MINT, PEPPERMINT, SPEARMINT NEW WORLD reds

NUTMEG

SAFFRON white dessert wines

THYME *Provençal* and *Languedoc* reds

VANILLA very common, from oak barrels

WHITE PEPPER *Grüner Veltliner*

BAKERY & DAIRY

Bread and yeast characteristics often appear in wines aged in contact with dead yeast cells from fermentation, such as Champagne. Buttery flavours are from malolactic fermentation, a secondary fermentation in which apple-like malic acid is converted to lactic acid, a component of milk.

BISCUIT *Champagne*

BREAD *Champagne*

BRIOCHE *demi-sec Champagne*

BUTTERY *Chardonnay*

CHEESE possible result of a BRETTANOMYCES fault

TOAST *Champagne*

YEAST *Muscadet Sur Lie*

tasting date: location:

tasting partner(s):

wine name:

producer:

region/appellation:

grape varieties:

vintage: alcohol: price:

COLOUR HUE:

WHITE: greenish | yellow | straw yellow | gold | amber
RED: purple | ruby | red | garnet | brick | brown
ROSÉ: pink | salmon | orange | copper

COLOUR DEPTH:
watery | pale | medium | deep | dark

CLARITY:
clear | slight haze | cloudy

AROMA INTENSITY:
low | moderate | aromatic | powerful

DEVELOPMENT:
youthful | some age | aged

AROMAS:

DRY/SWEET:
bone dry | dry | off dry | medium sweet | sweet | very sweet

BODY:
very light | light | medium | medium-full | full-bodied | heavy

ACIDITY:
tart | crisp | lively | smooth | flabby

TANNINS (IF PRESENT):
LEVEL: low | medium | high   TYPE: soft | round | dry | hard

FLAVOUR INTENSITY:
low | moderate | flavourful | powerful

FLAVOURS:

FINISH:
short (< 3 sec) | medium (4-5) | long (5-7) | v. long (>8 sec)

CONCLUSION/BALANCE:

rating:

FOOD: **FOOD PAIRING:**

MATCH: perfect | good | neutral | bad

tasting date: location:

tasting partner(s):

wine name:

producer:

region/appellation:

grape varieties:

vintage: alcohol: price:

COLOUR HUE:

WHITE: greenish | yellow | straw yellow | gold | amber
RED: purple | ruby | red | garnet | brick | brown
ROSÉ: pink | salmon | orange | copper

COLOUR DEPTH:
watery | pale | medium | deep | dark

CLARITY:
clear | slight haze | cloudy

AROMA INTENSITY:
low | moderate | aromatic | powerful

DEVELOPMENT:
youthful | some age | aged

AROMAS:

DRY/SWEET:
bone dry | dry | off dry | medium sweet | sweet | very sweet

BODY:
very light | light | medium | medium-full | full-bodied | heavy

ACIDITY:
tart | crisp | lively | smooth | flabby

TANNINS (IF PRESENT):
LEVEL: low | medium | high   TYPE: soft | round | dry | hard

FLAVOUR INTENSITY:
low | moderate | flavourful | powerful

FLAVOURS:

FINISH:
short (< 3 sec) | medium (4-5) | long (5-7) | v. long (>8 sec)

CONCLUSION/BALANCE:

rating:

FOOD: **FOOD PAIRING:**

MATCH: perfect | good | neutral | bad